4/11

G. Marie

Paul Austin

RETURN OF THE LOST ONE

Published in the United States by
Beckham Publications Group, Inc.
ISBN: 0-931761-93-X
10 9 8 7 6 5 4 3 2 1

RETURN OF THE LOST ONE

My Bout with Alcoholism

Paul A. Austin

THE Beckham
PUBLICATIONS GROUP, INC.

Silver Spring

Foreword

After reading this book, you might think that I have had too many chances at life. You might think that it is unfair for one person to turn down life so often, finally opt for success, and make it. I understand your feelings. Sometimes it seems remarkable to me myself that I am alive, healthy, and relatively happy.

I am 65 years old. I drank for 27 years of those years. And I spent four of those 27 years on skid row.

I had my last drink on June 8, 1972. On the next day, I entered DC Detox. Then, on June 12, I entered St. Elizabeth's Hospital, a mental institution in Washington, DC for treatment. There I spent 21 months on a locked ward for chronics. I was discharged on convalescent leave in early 1974. In 1976, I went to work in the field of alcoholism and drug addiction, and I have been there since.

In March 1985, I founded a counseling service with an outpatient treatment program certified by the State of Maryland for the treatment of alcohol and drug problems. As director, I employ 11 staffers including counselors, an

MD, PhD psychologists, an administrative assistant, an attorney, and a bookkeeper. *I have been sober now for over 30 years.*

As you read this book, you will see how important my ability to con and manipulate enabled me to survive. I hope you notice that alcoholism has many faces. Two faces are especially noteworthy. One is represented by the three to five percent of the alcoholics who can be readily identified as having a problem. But our society has difficulty identifying the second face—the other 95 percent who have a problem with alcoholism simply because their material gains—new cars, great jobs, lots of cash, and friends—insulate them from detection. We don't look at what is really going on in those people's lives. And as a consequence, many of them die not knowing what took them away.

Alcoholism is chronic. That means if you have it, you have it to keep. It never goes away. It is also progressive, so if you have it for any given time, it gets worse, never better. It is also fatal. Not treated, it can kill! It ranks fourth in our national fatality rate. It is of the same magnitude as heart disease, cancer, and mental disorders. It has tremendous negative impact on us all—from employees to loved ones.

If you believe you have a problem with alcoholism, seek help. Support is available in many places in our society. There is nothing to be ashamed of. Seeking help for a problem is healthy.   It is not a sign of moral degeneration or of weakness.   Some people just can't drink.

If you are not affected by alcoholism, please have compassion for your brothers and sisters who may be seeking a solution to this problem.   We need to understand more about what destroys our loved ones, our neighbors, our communities, and our society.

If you have a problem, do something about it. If you don't have a problem, I hope my story will act as a preventive measure.

Chapter 1

EARLY CHILDHOOD

The first night that I slept in my mother's arms, I was eleven months old. That was also the night that our log cabin burned down.

When she first saw the flames, she screamed out to my father, "There's a fire!" They jumped up and ran out with me in her arms. So I didn't get burned. Then they stopped. They discovered that my four sisters were still in the house. "The kids are still in there!" she shouted.

He rushed back to get them. The house was in a solid blaze. As he ran in, my two oldest sisters dashed past him. Suddenly he was caught under a burning, falling roof.

"Come through the window," my mother yelled, knocking out a window with her fist. He jumped through the window, head first. They hurried to the back of the house to one of the back windows (We only had about three or four windows in the whole house).

My father raised the window from the bottom and stuck his head under the smoke and fire and called out,

"Ossia, Opal!" He found Ossia standing by the window, and my father reached in and lifted her out to the safety of the ground. He grabbed Opal by the leg just as she was falling from the bed to the floor.

◆

I was the ninth child of my mother and father. There were twelve of us children altogether. My mother had four children when she married my father—two boys and two girls. The two boys went to live with other people. The first three children of my mother and father died— one brother, Adam Alphonsel; another brother, James Burlon; and a sister, Rosa Lee. They died shortly after birth.

My oldest sister, Ossia, was the oldest living child of my father. She was set in her ways; her own person who didn't listen much to anybody. Nor did she follow suggestions that were given to her. She would tell you what she thought both about herself and about you too. My mother always said that she didn't know much, but Ossia was like the mother of the household because she did most of the cleaning—when anything was cleaned. She did all of the cooking too. She was always a good cook. She just didn't take any stuff from anybody. Ossia didn't sulk over stuff; she just didn't give a damn. She didn't finish school. All of my brothers and sisters made it only to the eleventh grade. I was the exception; I completed high school.

Opal, my second oldest sister, was between Ossia and me. We always called her Niece. I think that nickname came from one of my father's half-sisters. Everybody seemed to be half-sisters and brothers, all mutts. Niece was a lot like me. She was a sensitive person who stayed to herself. She didn't like to get involved in anything that involved other people. She was lonely; liked being alone. She wouldn't defend herself. People picked on her, too. I guess that's why she meant so much to me, because I was the same way. I don't remember her doing much around the house. Ossia, not my mother, controlled the house. I think Niece just did what Ossia suggested.

I was the next born. After me came Silas. He was the "pet" or the spoiled brat. He was really mean and cruel. A lot of his meanness came through gestures and acting out, especially when he didn't get what he wanted or didn't get his way. He would be punished sometimes, but he didn't care about being punished.

My baby sister was Margaret Barbara Jean, but we always called her Katy. Katy was a nickname for one of my mother's relatives. She was the baby. Nobody bothered her at school because Silas was there, and he would fight anybody.

Katy and Ossia were the two children of the five belonging to my father. They resembled my father's family. All of us were skinny, except Ossia. Katy, as she grew up, grew stout, too. They, on the other hand, were big-boned people.

I was the first son of my father to live. I was born in Shady Grove, North Carolina, which is about three miles outside of Carthage. We would predict the seasons by the condition of our feet. If we were barefoot, then it was warm and not winter. If we were wearing four old socks and muddy boots, then it must be December, January, or February. That's how it was there in the early 1930s.

Many children died during those times because we didn't have access to physicians or dentists. I never knew a doctor until I was fourteen years old. Our medicine was from the woods—the herbs and the roots, rat vein, pine top tea, and others. Children were born at home with the aid of a midwife. Grandmas were there to help, too, as a rule. The midwife had worked half the day in the field already when she got the call to help my momma deliver me. I weighed eleven pounds at birth. After the midwife slapped me on the behind and I wailed, I slept for seven days! Everyone thought I was in a coma. But my grandma said, "He's just getting his business right." She must have known right then that I would be a unique case.

My momma said I was born with a kind disposition and that I changed after that. She always said that. I think I must have started acting and putting on a facade—

hiding the real Paul—from the start. No one knew the real me. I became an actor in my own life.

My parents always kept an eye on me. I guess because I was the oldest son of the marriage, I was close to my father. He was so proud of having a son who could follow him around and be with him.

During the day, little Silas, two years my junior, would beat the tar out of me. Silas was an evil little guy; they called him a devil when he was born because he was so mean. He didn't cry. He pouted. Silas beat up on me because I was available. He would attack anyone who came around, even adults. He hit my grandfather once with a brick. He attacked some grown-ups, who were my cousins, with rocks. Silas was left-handed, and it was hard to get away from a rock when he threw it at you because he could just make it curve and hit you upside the head.

Silas' beatings continued until I was fourteen—when I whipped him badly. One of the fears I had was that I would hurt him. So I didn't defend myself. I always felt that if I stepped out of line, I would lose control and I would really hurt somebody.

I never had a toy, but Silas got toys all the time. He would beat up on me, and my parents would buy *him* a toy. He got a brand new bicycle and a new red wagon and some smaller toys, and I never had a toy in my life. My mother always said that I was the nicest child she had and that I always listened to her. She said I was born with the mind of an adult, and I was above being a child anyway. She would say that I really shouldn't play as a child because my mind was so advanced.

I wanted to say to her, "But I am a child. I want to play. I want to have toys."

"Silas needs toys and you don't." She said that they didn't buy me toys because I would understand. But I didn't understand. You see, when I was growing up, you didn't back talk or cross words, because when they said something and looked at you and gave you that "sh" sign, that was it. You didn't question it. I think I was the most sensitive of the children. Maybe Opal was as sensitive as I am, but I was extremely sensitive and vulnerable. But mom said I was born with the mind of a mature man.

My mother said that at night I would walk and sing in my sleep. And one of the songs I would sing—and this is what she said, because I have no recollection—was "I'm Running for My Life." She would throw cold water on me to try to wake me. I also had nightmares.

I didn't understand fully the different types of feelings at that early age. But I do know that there was a tremendous amount of hurt and envy inside. I felt so worthless because Silas got those things and I didn't. My mother used to say that Silas would have things when he grew up, and I would never have anything. One of the reasons she said that was because I was too freehanded.

But there was a reason for that freehandedness. There were times when I would give what I had to make friends, to be a part of things—so somebody would like me. I did a lot of things so that I would be accepted. As I grew up, part of my personality was centered on pleasing people. I would do things that I thought people wanted me to do. I would respond when I learned that somebody was satisfied with the way I acted. I used to wake up sometimes, hearing my mom talking to dad: "Why don't you plough the garden, why don't you chop the garden, why don't you do this?" I would overhear these conversations that weren't meant for me. And the next morning when they got up, I was already doing it.

She would come out and tell me how great I was. I was the best child she had. I was highly praised. This grew into what I knew were high expectations of me. She made me do things when others wouldn't. I always would. It caused me so much pain. I learned to believe that my value to her depended upon what I would do. I got praised for doing well. If I fell short of what she thought I should do, I got a whipping. She always said to me that I was the best child she had and the only one who would listen to her. I should be punished because I knew better. The rest of them didn't, but I knew better.

I derived a great deal of pleasure from hitching up the mules or just watching over them. I used to lie down on my stomach on the dirt road outside our house and watch and study the mules' tracks for hours and days. I watched their hooves. I was fascinated by the tracks they made in the mud. I watched until I could recreate their hoof prints. I became a mule with the help of four tin cans. I bent one edge into itself until, when pressed down in the mud, it made the exact print of the mule's hoof. Being very careful not to let my own calves and feet touch the ground, I put on my hooves and trotted up and down our road. I became a mule with freedom of passage. The mules' wide, forlorn eyes also fascinated me.

I naturally compared the mule to the blacks, and the horse to the whites, when I started to hear things about distinguishing the races. The hair on them was different. The mule was powerful and strong with nappy, short hair. The horse was nice and fancy-shaped, frisky with a long mane. It was more sensitive. The mule was hardheaded. You had to get his attention by bopping him beside the head. There was a strong likeness in the way I thought in terms of blacks and whites, and mules and horses.

I was always told to be careful around whites; don't whistle, watch what you say. And, when you spoke with the horse, you spoke with the same kind of tone. You had to be gentle with the horse, because if you reared up with him, it made him nervous and sensitive. There has to be some comparison, but like I say again, I didn't understand my feelings—I didn't understand what was going on.

I imagine I liked the mule because his was so similar to my disposition. The mule was unpredictable. It was pointed out to me by grown-ups, "Be careful around a mule because he'll watch you and as soon as he thinks he's got you hemmed up, he'll hurt you." My personality turned out to be the same. I became unpredictable. I never knew what I was going to do next.

I needed an emotional hookup, and the mules provided that emotional link. I had no emotional link at the school, I had no emotional link at the church, and I had no emotional link at home—except for the emotional bond that I had with my sister, Niece. We were sensitive people, and we stayed to ourselves. We could feel that we needed some kind of protection, so we depended on each other to support our fears.

My father loved me; I could feel that. But we never had a man-to-man talk. I never understood anything about life itself, and my role in it or my direction. It was just all information from long distance that I overheard, that I manufactured and tried to turn around to make some sense out of it. I was ashamed or embarrassed to discuss some of the things that I overheard because I didn't know if it was right or not. I don't think the morals were too strict back then, and some of that looseness rubbed off on me, too. Everybody was having babies, and the first thing the adults wanted to do was jump on the bandwagon and tell you these things were wrong. The girls' having all of these babies was a way of getting attention, getting rid of some of their frustrations. They weren't taught not to or how to protect themselves, because back then talking about those kinds of things was taboo. I'm really talking about the parents; they were having all these babies. The result: you'd have all kinds of half this and half that, and everybody around was a cousin. Everybody I talked to was my cousin.

Later on in my life I would have fantasies about those gals that I went to school with because they were so pretty. They didn't know it, but I was sitting back looking.   But every time I would look at a woman, somebody would come up and tell me that she was Uncle Johnny's sister, Suzie's daughter—which would make her my cousin.

"You can't look at her."

Well whom do you look at? Everybody was related. They never talked about sex, what to do and how to protect yourself, or what can happen to you as a result of it. They quoted from the Bible—Adam and Eve in the Garden, hiding behind fig leaves, Adam eating the apple off the tree, and man being punished ever since. You had to go and multiply and replenish the earth; that was what man was put here for.

So my parents told me that kids come out of stump holes. I was always looking in the woods, looking for babies in stump holes in the woods. They didn't say where the stump holes were, but I knew what a stump hole was—the bottom of a tree that's rotted, and I was looking in these stumps to see if there were any babies in there. I saw possums in there, but no babies.

♦

My sister tells me that I began singing before I was five. She dragged me along to church, and while she pulled on my arm, I would sing to her. Actually my sister also said that as far back as she can remember, I was an unusual child, and started to sing when I was around two. Holding her hand, dragging my toes, I would be singing, "Rock My Soul in the Bosom of Abraham." But I couldn't say the words clearly; they would come out slurred. This is one of the things that led me to church, I guess—much more than anything else.

It was my mother again: "Paul is the nicest one, so I had to put more into him than the others." So I went to church regularly.

I hated church. I hated the preacher. I hated the people. My mother always pushed me out in the front. But I couldn't let anyone know about my hatred, because, after all, I was "Miss Phoebe's son," and I was nice. I had to make the proper observances and conform to the social graces of the church. I had to say hello to the preacher and to all the other Methodists. And I had to do this not only on Sundays, but also on every other day of the week. My mother had "found God," and somehow I had not, and I was, therefore, a SINNER. I was a sensitive child, and many times I would be crying while I was shaking hands with everyone. I didn't like those moments, but my mother made me, and I didn't know why. Every time they prayed—and it seemed an endless process, believe me—I had to go up front to get prayed for. I didn't like people looking at me. I guess that is what started much of my paranoia—a phenomenon I didn't even recognize until I started my recovery from alcohol. It was the beginning of the tightness in my chest, the sweating, and the veins around my temples popping out. Everybody was watching me. I could feel the blood running through my head. I had to go up and expose myself to all of this kind of stuff.

Those preachers did a lot of things I didn't approve of. But still they would always remind me of where I was going (to hell) if I didn't do things right and think right, or if I had any bad thoughts.

So it was natural that I was scared to death if I had any thoughts about a woman. I knew that thoughts about adultery or of going to bed with a woman would send me to hell. I was trying to make myself not think about women, but the thoughts would come.

I watched these women involved in these great revelations. They drank booze and sat around when the men were at work. These old women—saints they called themselves—wore high-top shoes with stockings and long dresses. One day I was looking at one woman's ankles; I guess I was just looking at the shoes, but my mom thought that I was trying to look up the woman's dress. I had no intention of looking under her dress; I was looking at those shoes. She said, "Boy, what you doing trying to look up that woman's dress?" From then on, I was very curious about what it was she was trying to keep me from seeing.

These are some of the things that caused me to have so much resentment for people in the church. They never explained. I never could talk about what I thought. How could I identify any feelings if I could never talk about them? When I was growing up, children were to be seen and not heard. When adults said something, that's what went, no matter what it was. If you had a stomachache and you cried, it would be good if you didn't tell them what you were crying about, because they weren't going to listen anyhow.

Every Sunday we were on our way to church. My mother was concerned about the personal prestige—the high and mighty and the rolling of the head—that's where she was going. She loved us, I know, as best she could, but I really didn't need all that stuff. And one of the things that upset me was that my mom would collect money for things that were going on at the church. My father would say, "Phoebe, don't you ask them people for money, that embarrasses me; you beg too much." That made me angry because I knew he was hurting. And I was frustrated because it always kept happening.

The preacher or somebody from the church would be invited to the house when we had good food on Sunday: chicken and dumplings, gravy and cabbage, eggplant, corn on the cob. My mother would spend a great deal of time and pain in the kitchen on Sundays fixing special meals for those people. I didn't like that, but I would grin, and I couldn't tell her I didn't like that. While they were eating, all of us kids would sit on the porch looking through the screen door, watching these people eat all of the best parts of the chicken—the breast and the legs, and sopping up all the gravy with the hot biscuits. They were more important than we were. We were the kids, and I always wondered why these people got the best food. She's telling them, "Paul and the kids like the chicken feet and the necks." I didn't like the feet and the necks; I wanted what those people were eating, but I had to put on this face and smile and pretend that I did like them. No wonder I didn't have any great love for the church. But the people thought I did. I just gave the impression that I did, because if they respected and had consideration for other people, they wouldn't have watched us kids sit out there and wait while they ate the best because a mother said that the kids could eat this.

I know my kids aren't going to do that. I resented my mother for giving the good food to the church people. The impression I always got was that she thought more of these people than she did of me. This was always where her personal prestige was examined—it was the view the church had of Phoebe and her fine children. She was also saying, too, that she was the best child of her mother. She had twelve siblings—five boys and seven girls. She said she was the best child her father and mother had. I always thought if she's the best one, the others must be real jerks.

As a preschool sinner in Shady Grove, one has certain rights—the right to be wetted up periodically with a pail of water; the right to attend far too many prayer meetings in order to be prayed over by those who had somehow miraculously "found God," and the right to sit on the "mourner's bench"—a special place reserved for sinners like me.

This was all extremely confusing. Being under five years of age, I was treated like a child. No one would tell me the reasons behind any of this frantic activity. It supposedly, to my young mind, had something to do with saving my soul. But nobody told me what my soul was or where it was. I got the impression that I had been born with a broken one, however, and that others had had these broken mysterious things, too. Somehow my mother's broken mysterious object had gotten fixed because she had talked with, and had heard from, and had been touched by a large old man called God. I wondered if this big old man named God was anything like my father. It never occurred to me to ask him how he did it. Did this mean that I had to do what my mother had done so I, too, could lose the brand of sinner? What exactly had she done? She would not tell me. She only took me to more prayer meetings.

I pondered all of this in my clear, objective, fully informed five-year-old mind. I weighed the evidence of my mother's behavior and her words. I knew the humiliation of "being saved." All of those people—and especially the preacher—looking at me, and praying over me, and drowning me day after day, were putting me in pure torture. The preacher's eyes had become laser beams. The people's voices had become sirens. The pails of water had become tidal waves. The jury, in my mind, came back with the verdict: GUILTY, and it's too confusing to change. I would keep the brand of sinner, play along with the crowd, and get out as soon as possible.

Bob Marshall Farm:
I assisted in hooking up my first mule to a wagon in 1942.

Chapter 2

DEPENDENCY

My mother burned my moral education into me. I was a victim of sin and wages, and I felt the impending doom. I felt a different kind of doom as she took me by the hand along the old dirt road by the old lynch tree one day. We walked that way to church, and she always took me with her. There was a huge, old tree with a limb hanging over the road.

"That's the lynch tree," she would say—nothing more. But, in my mind, the explanation rang, "Black men dead!" Why? White women? I was beginning to understand that sin had something to do with black and white mixing—and in a certain way. We were associated with farming, and I could play with the white boys in the field when we were working, but I could not play with the little girls! No, no, no! Good God, I might not only suffer a terrible physical death from playing with the white girls, but I would also surely be sentenced to an eternal fate worse than my current life!

I liked those cotton fields and the scavenging for sweet potatoes and buttermilk from the workers. Why couldn't I drink from the same water? Why couldn't I play with both sexes of those white folks?

Wayside School: I entered school in 1942 at five years old.

When I turned five in 1942 I started primer school—what we call kindergarten today.   Oh, the pain of separation!   I faced my greatest fears that year. I was taken from mom and dad, away from the mules, and sent to school—straight into the arms and strange words of nurses who vaccinated me. The smell of the clinic scared me to death. Those white hands held big needles and told me that it wouldn't hurt. They lied! It hurt like hell.

I wanted to run back to my house—to my mules. Those animals were my greatest friends, my greatest inspiration—so strong in their pulling the ploughs. I loved the hollering that sounded like music: "Woo," for stop; "Gee," for going to the left; "Haw," for go right. Those round hooves plodded, and the long ears heard everything. The eyes made quick right-left movements, always looking around. Mules are stubborn, but they listen. Their tails and manes are kinky and need special trimming. But the mule will wait to carry out his revenge for a hurt, and he won't damage himself in the process. I watched the horses, too, but they were not worthy of my admiration. Their manes and tails flowed too long and were different shades of colors. The horses panicked, and if a horse would try to harm you, he'd probably hurt himself in the process.

So, I was dragged off to school. Of course it was segregated, with ages from six to thirteen in one schoolhouse.

The other kids in school had neat, clean, store-bought clothes. Mine were made out of fertilizer sacks. My mother is as good a seamstress as the best, but I felt terrible wearing those homemade clothes dyed with inks from the five-and-ten-cent store. The other kids had animal crackers and peanut butter and jelly sandwiches. I had greasy cornbread stuffed with homemade butter, wrapped in saved brown paper scraps. I wouldn't let anyone see what I had for lunch. I hid my awful packet in my back pocket. I refused to store it on the lunch bag shelf. At break time, I ran out back and stood alone up on the hill in the woods to eat my food, which by this time had stained my seat and the rear of my trousers. After the teacher rang the cowbell, I'd come back to the building. I was terrified that the others would beat me up for being so ugly and different. My neck was too long, my ears stuck out, and my mother's food and clothing marked me as an outcast. I was socially and physically unworthy. Now, in school, I realized that not only God, but also my peers, would shut me out forever.

My clothes were made from the white fertilizer sacks we used to grow tobacco. My mother would rip them and make clothes. She could really stitch, just as good as a sewing machine. She would make our high bib overalls from those sacks and dye them blue, but you could still tell they were homemade. The paranoia and the consciousness of my having to wear these things—and my thinking that people were looking at them (maybe they actually liked them, who knows?)—led me to believe that they didn't like me so they didn't like what I was wearing either.

We only got about one pair of shoes a year. The bottoms had the imprint of a tire track. Sometimes I would make a track and start backing up and looking at the track on the ground. We had to wear those shoes for all the seasons—they were church shoes, school shoes, and everyday shoes. My mother's primary reason now for the food and the clothes was to protect us; it was the way she loved us. If there were other kids in the school who dressed the same way, I didn't see them. When you were filled with the kind of dread and anxiety that I had, you don't see other people's problems. You're just tuned in on yourself, and I hadn't identified what this was all about anyway.

What I knew is that they had taken me away from the mules, the farm, and my dad to go to school, and I was sitting there scared to death. I was afraid to put my hand up, I was wetting my pants, and I was sitting on my lunch as grease came through my pants. The kids looked at me as if I were something good to eat—somebody they could fight. They saw my vulnerability and sensitivity, and they were already attacking me with their eyes. So, I had to run at school, and then run at home because I would also get beat up there by my brother, Silas. Between the time I entered school and about eight years old, I was so emotionally and mentally confused and frightened to death that I didn't know how to act or what to do.

God's will had been drilled into me. God wanted no parts of anything bad. You had to be pure and clean and righteous, and I wasn't that—certainly when considering the way that I was treated. I was treated with cold cruelty, and it hurt. It was painful. The kids looked at me and treated me with scorn. Then my brother, Silas was punishing me at home. And when I wasn't 100 percent perfect performing my chores, I got it from my mother. She said that she had put more work into me and that I should know better; so I should do things differently. I was going through hell. So why should God care about me?

Then, when I was eight, we moved closer to Carthage, where I entered Pinkney High. This was a school where *all* grades went, from first through twelfth. My fears grew greater. Moving me to a new school was like taking a fish out of water. I was faced with a new environment and some new people again. I hoped the kids would be my friends. Instead, the Pinkney kids treated me the same way that the kids at Wayside School had.

Something had to suffer for the way I was suffering. So, why not make the animals suffer? I began to kill dogs and cats. It seemed fair to me: skin it, cut it, or do something to make it suffer since it was one of those who was always after me.

The first dog I killed was the one that old man Vic gave me. He told me it was a tree dog. But it had little short ears, and I had always known tree dogs to have long ears. I carried the dog home with me, walking through the yard where loose chickens were laying eggs everywhere. He found a nest of chicken eggs that we had been looking for. Every time I had done something wrong, they wanted to baptize me again to cleanse me. I would cleanse the dog because he had found the hen's nest.

Some other boys from the neighborhood had come over to see the dog. "Help me put the dog in a sack," I said. "Let's drag him down to the river."

I think the others came along just to see if it was really going to happen. The river had a bridge over it, so we tied a rope to the sack and dropped it over the side of the bridge, still holding onto the rope. "We are going to cleanse it," I said, then uttered a prayer as I dropped him in the water, just as they had done to me. It was always said that when they baptized me it was to make me a better person, so maybe this would also apply to the dog. We pulled the dog up and then let him back down into the river.

"Look at the bubbles coming up through the water," somebody laughed. I didn't know at the time, but this was my way of expressing fear and hostility.

In this new school, I met a new group of kids who were just as mean to me. "You look like you from Mars," they laughed, thumping my head every chance they got. They would gang up on me after school and pummel me with their fists until I lay there on the ground, beaten and crying.

One day a senior named Austin, big, black and hefty breasts, saw me crying and ran over to me. She kneeled down beside me. She put my head under her breast and stroked my head with kindness. It felt warm and I felt totally protected. I didn't know that this would begin a long process for me of being dependent. Every time something happened, I would be looking for someone to bail me out of trouble.

Her rescuing me would happen often. I even looked for it to happen. Sometimes the kids had not bothered me at all. But I would still put on the act so that my friend who had adopted me would lay my head against her breast and stroke my head. I didn't know then, but I know now that addiction to alcoholism is rooted in a similar kind of dependency.

You must find something that feels good...warm...caressing. I didn't know it then, but I was becoming dependent on this girl. She gave me what I had always wanted—to be warm and touched. Who wouldn't like to be warm like that? Strangely, I would be looking for those guys to beat up on me so I could be rescued. Years later, as an alcoholic, I believed that it was all right to get drunk because there would be a detox to go to.

I took her name and made it part of mine. The name given to me at birth was William Paul Alston (W.P.A.). I hated that name. The W.P.A. was something bad, for me and everyone else. Those were the initials for the Works Progress Administration, a government relief program for poor people is the way I understood it. Later on in life, I would change my name to Paul Augustus Austin, taking the last name of the high school girl who protected me. She protected me as long as she could—until she finished school—and I was alone again. My anger and hostility returned, and I reverted to killing dogs and cats. I didn't like killing dogs because I loved them and they would hunt for us. But the kids at school were beginning to lean on me, so I continued my role of executioner.

Chapter 3

MY FIRST DRINK

I was eight when I had my first drink. I was tagging along with Dad when we went to Mitchell's place. A farmer like the rest of the men, Mitchell also raised grapes, big fat scuppernongs, from which he made the best wine in the county and sold it to my father and his friends.

"Mitch, let the boy here have a swig of those grapes," my father said.

"Sure, but just a taste. An' you oughta be careful; the next thing you know, that boy'll be after a taste of all the sweet stuff you buy."

The men broke out into laughter, slapping their thighs and each other's hands, teasing my father. I didn't know why. After their fun with Dad, they began drinking, sucking the wine up from a jar. They used an old hose; the same kind we drew gas out of trucks and trailers with. When they turned their heads and were paying no attention, I drew wine through that hose. I did it about three times, until I thought my stomach would bust wide open.

"That's enough, boy." Dad's voice no longer had its laughter. "Bring your narrow behind over here and let's go home."

We didn't go home. Dad took me to the barn to rest.

"And keep your drunk self quiet until I come back. I told you to take just one taste. Your mama find out, she gone kills us."

I was annoyed that we had left Mitchell's place. Why? I felt good. I wasn't afraid of anything or anybody. I felt tough and strong, as if I could "fight lions with a switch"—just as Little Willie John said in his song. I stood up to fight those lions. I screamed at them and dared them. Then, there was a slow fade to black. I passed out. I behaved like this for another twenty-seven years.

In addition to getting drunk for the first time at age eight, I also, for the first time, dipped snuff and chewed tobacco. Brown Mule Chewing Tobacco had a strong kick, just like a mule. Dad gave me some. I think he figured if I chewed enough and got sick, it would turn me against chewing tobacco. He was half right. My stomach churned. A queasiness crept through my body, and finally I threw up.

"Want any more tobacco?" Dad asked, smiling.

"Yes sir, just don't give me any with the mule on it."

We laughed about that for many years.

But tobacco got my father's eye put out that same year. We were housing tobacco, hanging it in on tiers from the barn roof so we could cure it with heat. We built a log fire and sprinkled sawdust on it so the log wouldn't burn so fast and we could get a lot of heat. There are furnaces built into the barn, but if you don't know how to raise the heat just right, the tobacco stems won't completely cure, and they will be swollen. Some of those stems did swell, so we took that tobacco to the house to see if we could dry up the stems. Damn it, there was nothing in the roof to hang the tobacco on.

"If we don't have bad luck, we don't have luck at all," Dad said. "Let's get up in the loft and build some makeshift tiers to hang this tobacco on. I need to get these stems dried up."

I held the end of an old warped piece of wood while Dad drove a nail. Just as the hammer hit the nail head, the nail ricocheted like a silver missile heading straight for Dad's eyes. It hit him in the middle of the left eye. Fluid poured out from it. The nail cut the nerves, killing them, and that is why I think Dad didn't scream.

I grabbed his hand—it was sweaty and trembling—and led him straight down an old ladder. A neighbor took him to Pinehurst Hospital and then to Duke Hospital in Durham. At Duke, doctors removed my father's eye.

While they operated on Dad's eye at Duke, I was in Pinehurst Hospital, put there by George, the most stubborn mule in the world. He knew I couldn't handle him so he waited until he had a clear shot before he bolted and ran away. I pulled back on the reins as hard as I could, but I wasn't strong enough to hold him. I kept yelling "whoa" and he kept running. The wagon shot over a hill, overturned and threw a load of tobacco and me to the ground. The wagon's back wheel ran over the back of my foot. Neighbors took me to Pinehurst Hospital with bruises and a crushed heel.

While Dad and I recovered in our separate hospitals, our tobacco crop over ripened; "burned up," we call it. We were sharecroppers and our crop was burning up in the field. The man we farmed for planned to put us off his farm. It didn't matter whose fault it was that we were in the hospital. We weren't putting the tobacco in, and that was the bottom line—no tobacco, no money.

Dad expected the landlord's decision. We usually moved every two or three years from farm to farm anyway, sharecropping. As I look back over a half-century, I see now that poverty was the only constant thing in our lives.

♦

Birthdays and Christmases were very painful and sad occasions for me. I had the Christmas Spirit but not Christmas toys, bikes and goodies. I didn't get any of the things my friends enjoyed. So I told lies about what Santa had left under the tree for me. But my Christmas tree was really the city dump, which was within walking distance. I went there to find shoes and clothes that I could wear to school.   My constant fear was that someone would recognize his shirt or pants or socks and point them out to the entire class. Or another might discover where I had shopped for my wardrobe and expose me.

That wasn't all I found out there on the outskirts of the city. I also discovered bags of liquor bottles at the dump. Like a pharmacist, I drained each bottle I found into a one-pint size until I had a good shot's worth to pour down my throat. I swaggered away from the dump feeling terrific—smiling to myself, reminding myself of how ingenious I was, even looking for someone or something to attack. This ritual of discovery and inebriation went on—before I knew it, I could count five years.

My dad and I went past the dump and into the forest to cut wood so that we can sell it. It was hard work that left our shoulders aching. Finished, we hauled the wood to Pinehurst and sold it for five dollars. Selling was the fun part because Dad sang out: "Fresh Wood! Fresh Wood!" I laughed at his funny tune. After a sale, Dad bought us a dollar's worth of orange slice candy. I loved my father, and I knew he loved me too, although he didn't tell me often. I guess it wasn't manly to say, "I love you" out loud. Maybe Dad felt it was a kind of weakness. With his one-eyed self, he would reach over and tickle me.

Arriving back home, I imagine we looked like Sylvester the cat after he swallows Tweetie bird. Our mouths are rife with the taste and smell of orange slice candy, while Mother's and the kids' are white from hunger. Mother's brow was wrinkled, her face taut, and her eyes filled with . . . I think she was mad at us.

Getting food for her to cook was rarely a problem. Much of it came from the woods—rabbits, squirrels, and even crows. I love hunting. I started when I turned thirteen and killed my first squirrel. Pride overtook me and I hauled that squirrel around in Dad's old Chevrolet truck for two or three days, showing it to neighbors and friends. When the excitement was gone, it was time to eat the squirrel; but one thing had happened—it had rotted.

One day I was down near the swamp where I had just shot two crows. On the way home, I passed a country barber.

"What's that you got in your bag?" he asked.

"Nothing but some wild swamp chickens."

"Look here boy, if you give me them chickens, I'll give you the best haircut you ever had."

I took him up on his offer, handed him the bag, and watched him smile with satisfaction. I didn't see him again until about two weeks later.

"Paul, you know those two swamp chickens you traded me?"

"Yes sir."

"Well, I burned up a whole wood pile trying to cook those chickens."

Crows are real tough to cook. We had a big laugh.

Although the woods gave us game to eat, our other meat came from the hogs, goats, and chickens we raised. Once I even lived with the chickens.

I was big for my age and so was my attitude. At nine, I worked in tobacco fields just like the men—pegging tobacco, hoeing weeds, and pulling suckers for 25 cents an hour. Mom took what little money I made, and I didn't like that worth a damn. It seemed that everybody just sat back and waited for me to bring something to eat, something to spend, or something to beat my behind with. To hell with that! I moved out of the house and set up quarters in the chicken shack. I sat on the wet ground looking at chicken droppings everywhere. Then I saw a black snake lurking outside, waiting his chance to crawl inside and suck up the chicken eggs.

"You don't scare me, Mr. Snake," I warned, rising above the swishing broom... "You don't scare me, Mr. Snake"...splashing water..."You don't scare me, Mr. Snake." Squawking chickens were flying all over the place. "I'm gonna clean this place and you're gonna get your tails out of here." When the last chicken flew out, I made a hanging bed with some blankets. With my new place ready, I went to the store to pick up some food—cans of sardines, Vienna sausages, and potted meat with bread or crackers—and headed home. I passed the main house.

"How y'all doing?"

"Fine! How you?" Mom and Dad laughed, shaking their heads.

I didn't care. I went to the chicken house and put my food along the walls, pulled a chair outside and sat down. I lived there only during the day because at night I was too afraid of the dark.

♦

My father was six feet, three inches tall, straight soft, fluffy hair. Women liked to touch his hair; roll it around their fingers while smiling seductively at him. I watched women stare at him while he and some of his friends were drinking. They liked him because of his hair, I thought. If my hair were curly like his, they'd like me, too. Damn! I wish I had good hair. Maybe then women would look at me, touch my hair, and love me.

Mr. TC, a man in Carthage, was well known for his conkalines, or his variation of a conk. Cab Calloway and Malcolm X—when he was a small-time hustler—made that slick, greasy imitation of straight hair popular. Mr. TC used a concoction of white potatoes and Red Devil lye to make his conks. I asked him to conk my hair although I knew it would last only two weeks. If you didn't get another one right away, your hair turned red from the lye.

Then gnats and flies, attracted by the grease, flashed all around your head.

After I got my conk, people laughed at me to my face. That hurt my feelings. I just wanted to be part of something, to love someone, and have someone to love me—claim me. Well, they all could just go to hell. After a taste of corn liquor, or some home brewed wine, I felt better, tougher. They could all kiss my ass. Who needed them anyway? I pulled out my knife and looked for some stray animal.

Chapter 4

BECOMING A MAN—OR SO I THOUGHT—AT FOURTEEN

I started working at the sawmill when I was fourteen. I smeared tar on my bibbed overalls so that I would look older. My first job at the sawmill was carrying "slabs," the rough bark cut away from felled trees. I desperately wanted another job because the slabs scarred my arms.

Finally, I got one. My new job was in the woods, away from the sawmill. When I first got to the woods and saw George, the runaway mule that caused my foot to be crushed, I was a little nervous.

I was "snaking" logs. You snaked, or moved logs around, with a can hook and a mule. It was tricky because they didn't tell you how to direct the mule. You had to talk the mule through his maneuvers using a kind of singsong talk. And he'd follow your directions.

You told him what to do and he popped those logs and lined them up in a pile. *"Get up there...hawwww; move now, come on; come on, I said, get; Hold it!"*

Sometimes it was frustrating, but I loved directing mules to snake logs and pile them so that a tractor could pick the logs up and carry them into the mill.

"Why you smiling all the time?" one of the workers asked me.

"Because I enjoy my work," I said.

Eventually I got a chance to do a little of everything out there in the woods— except drive tractors and haul logs. I might have done that too, but the boss called me back to the mill to "trip lumber." That's when you kick the can hooks off the carriage that brought the logs to the mill to be sawed. Nine times out of ten, it was my cousin doing the sawing. That was one crazy man. Sometimes he had that saw smoking he was running so many logs through. They put me behind him turning logs. I was excited by the need for precise timing. When my cousin pushed and shifted the logs the other way (reversed them) he took off the can hooks and it was my job to get them and trip, or hook, the logs as they went back through. It was exciting and I think that I matured with the responsibility.

I made a little money and on payday I went straight home—had to—and gave my mother an accounting of what I made. Fortunately, before I got home, I had already spent most of my paycheck at the side store buying sardines, pork and beans, crackers, Pepsi Colas, and Johnnycakes. Then I went home for the accounting.

At the front door, she said, "Boy, where's that money?"

I gave it to her.

"It's my money anyway, because you're mine," she said. There was no cheer in her voice.

Sometimes, if I was lucky, I got thirty-five cents back for what we called the picture show—twenty-five cents to get into the movie and ten cents for popcorn. At the movies, I watched reels and reels of Hop-A-Long Cassidy in "North of the Rio Grande" and "Heart of Arizona." I remember Roy Rogers in "Wild Horse Rodeo" and Lash LaRue in "Outlaw Country."

I was angry about my mother's behavior. I'd already moved into the chicken house. Even at fourteen, I thought she was wrong for taking my money, and I thought she was wrong, too, with her babble about turning the other cheek. That's the way God wants it, she taught.

"Get God to take care of those who do wrong to you," she preached to us.

That attitude angered and confused me. People were beating up on me, and all she wanted me to do was "leave it in the hands of the Lord." In the meantime, I'm getting black eyes and bruises. I felt so trapped, like that dog I had wrapped up to punish. Why should I take all of that punishment?

It was during this time that I began to realize that the God who was going to punish those who wronged me had prepared me to take care of myself. I had waited all those years, until I was fourteen, to believe that I should defend myself. I had my first fight with my brother Silas.

He, three of my sisters, and I walked home from school. We lived about two miles from the schoolhouse. When we were half way home we jostled for position before tearing into a run. The first one in the house would be able to eat the most. I was the fastest of us all and they knew it. I had honed my track skills by running from schoolmates chasing me. My sisters and brother knew I would be the one to eat the most. I ate anything, as if I were some kind of garbage disposal. If it were lying around, I'd eat it. When my brothers and sisters left food on their plates, my father told them not to worry.

"Just leave it on the table. Paul will get it," he chuckled.

On this day coming home, we started watching each other at the halfway mark, trying to anticipate who was going to make the break first. Before I knew what happened, Silas kicked me and then threw a rock at Katy.

I grabbed him by his shirt collar and hit him in the face with short, quick punches. I was so frustrated and full of emotion that I was almost crying. I kept pummeling him, feeling my knuckles penetrate the soft skin of his cheeks. I beat him something terrible. I didn't want to stop. Suddenly, God had given me the power to take care of myself and I had to show Silas that I could. For almost fourteen years, I had feared that if I fought him, I wouldn't turn him loose before I really hurt him. I finally let go of him, and he staggered away from me, his eyes wide and startled.

The five of us continued on home. We didn't run that day; we walked full of surprise and anger as we looked at each other wondering what had just happened.

We finally got to the house and climbed the flight of steps to the front porch, opened the door and walked in. I was the first one in. It must have been a strange sight to my father. We usually hit the door scrambling and screaming to get in. Dad, suffering from asthma real bad, was sitting on the far side of the room. He wasn't real active—he just sat around. No sooner than I got into the room, Silas hauled off and kicked me in the behind. Bolstered by my newfound attitude, I turned around, snatched Silas and threw him across the room. He hit the wall and slid to the floor as if he were a broken dummy. I didn't care.

My dad didn't know what was going on. He had never before seen me defend myself against Silas or anyone else. He jumped up and stood between us, trying to stop whatever had gotten into us. Silas reached around him and hit me in the jaw. I crawled between Dad's legs, rose and hit Silas in the face again, busting him up sure enough this time. Blood trickled down his cheeks, and he had a knot on his forehead as big as a rock for a week. That was the last fight Silas and I ever had.

♦

Shortly after that, I broke my left foot while playing at school. The old Pickney High School had burned down, but all of the debris from the fire had been left behind the new school. We played out there in the schoolyard, stepping over the glass, nails, and splintered wood. Somehow while playing, I fractured my foot. At the time, I didn't know it was fractured and walked on it for three days, allowing the blood to get into the bone marrow. Pretty soon, I had an infection.

Doctors put a cast on my foot, but after a week my foot swelled, sending sharp darts of pain up my leg. They removed the cast, but my foot continued swelling. The doctor had to operate. The whole thing was one big, painful experience. I stayed out of school for almost a year and did my school work at home. I wore out three pairs of crutches with that broken foot.

Since I was home, my mother arranged for me to baby-sit. But that stint as a babysitter didn't work out. I was too devilish. Once I wrote on the wall: "I broke my damn foot, now what do you want to do about it?" I don't know to whom the question was addressed. Nor do I understand why I frightened those little kids who were under my charge.

For example, I found a coconut with a face carved on it resembling a monkey. It had eyes made out of stone—colored and all. I carried this monkey face home and used it to frighten the children. I took a rope and tied one end to the coconut and the other end to the kid's leg I was babysitting. Then I went into another room.

"Come in here where I am," I yelled to the little boy.

He started walking, and as soon as he took his first steps, the monkey's head came out from behind him, and he had a fit. When his parents came to pick him up, I wanted them to think I was such a nice babysitter so I yelled for the kid to come here and play with me. He ran like crazy, looked back at me, and yelled: "Monk. Monk. Monk."

I acted as if I didn't know what was wrong with the kid. That whole scene tickled me to death. Eventually, the parents got someone else to watch their child. They said the kid was afraid of me.

♦

I was growing up and wanted people to feel like me. I wanted to be a man. When hair began to grow around my mouth to form a mustache, I could feel the manhood coming. Once I started shaving, I really thought I had arrived; I was my own man—drinking and shaving. Smoking came right after shaving, thanks to my mother.

"If he can shave, then he can smoke also," she said one day, more from anger than anything else.

I had been smoking, but not openly. When I had been a very young boy, Dad let me roll his homemade cigarettes. I used paper and Prince Albert smoking tobacco. In the process of making the cigarettes, I would take a puff. So I was already smoking, but not with my parents' blessing. With my mother's knowledge, I began smoking. I had arrived.

I worked at the sawmill, wore bibbed overalls like old men, and carried my lunch in four-pound lard buckets. I smoked, drank hard liquor and now was shaving. I had been driving since I was 13, not legally, but for my father, because we were farmers. When the police saw, me they turned their heads. Younger guys looked at me as if I was somebody. "Drinking and smoking, living in a fool's paradise," is the line to an old blues song, but there was trouble in paradise because of my foot. It wouldn't heal.

The hospital doctors began to insinuate that my foot should be amputated. In the end, they removed and replaced a bone in my foot. Ironically, I was angry when they replaced the bone. I found out there was some kind of insurance, or some little kiddy fund, or something associated with the school that would have paid me $125 if I had lost my foot. One hundred and twenty-five dollars! I had already figured it out. I would spend $25 on a peg leg and have $100 cash left. That would make me the richest black boy in the South, certainly in my community. But this doctor saved my foot by changing the bone, cutting me out of my $125. I was hot as hell with him. I wanted to kill him.

That's where my head was at that time. I had a lot of time to think about what I wanted to do. Going to school was not in the plan. Not one of my brothers or sisters had completed high school. It didn't appeal to me either. I planned to drop out of school when I became sixteen and wouldn't be required to attend. I didn't make it. I dropped out at fifteen.

The truancy officers were looking for me and I knew what that meant—maybe the Army. That's what they did back in those days. If you didn't work or go to school, you were drafted into the Army. There was no hanging around on the corners, so I returned to school and to the same grade. I had no intentions of finishing school. The teachers and principal put me into the next grade and encouraged me to continue, but to no avail.

My dad was sick. Although he was only 48, he needed me to help him on the farm so that we would have some place to live. That was another reason that I didn't want to attend school. I was afraid and ashamed that someone might learn about my dirt-poor family situation.

Mr. Gordon W. Herring, called "Horse" by grownups, was my agriculture teacher. He liked me, I think, because I was a farmer. He called me half-Ross—my mother's maiden name was Ross. It felt good that someone noticed me. Mr. Herring was the greatest influence in my life in terms of school attendance. I became involved in agriculture, and began to get some positive attention from people. Since I was farming, I did well in agriculture classes. I also participated in club activities requiring parliamentary procedure. I learned how to conduct meetings and put things on the shelf—table them, and take them off the table.

I even formed a singing group, the NFA (New Farmers of America) Quartet. I also judged livestock. The quartet was so good (and so was my livestock judging), it took second place out of seventeen groups with 200 boys in the Southern region.

The quartet went to A&T College in Greensboro, North Carolina, for one week during each of my four years in high school. We always appeared at the main auditorium. There were fourteen groups in competition that went through a process of elimination until only two remained. We came out winners for four years. Many people said that our final competitors had as much talent as we did except for one area—my bass singing. They didn't have anyone who topped my bass. This group experience was actually my introduction to first-rate singing. The quartet even appeared on television in Greensboro.

Finally, I was doing things that I enjoyed. People were looking at me with respect. I had figured people didn't like me, but now things were changing. I still drank every weekend, but no one noticed my behavior, I thought. I acted comically when drinking—telling stories and cutting up—and people liked to have me around them. They would even pay for my drinks. All the myths about drinking and what it will do for you sounded very good to me then, but they didn't tell it all!

I had a good, close relationship with the other members of the NFA Quartet, but my drinking puzzled them. I would never drink before a performance. But afterwards I wanted, needed a drink.

"Let's get a drink," I said as casually as I could.

"We don't want a drink and why do you?" they replied.

"I just thought maybe you wanted a drink and, since I thought you wanted one, I'll just get me one."

It was a lame reason to excuse the alcoholism that had already made its mark on me. I was having a drink because I actually thought I needed one. I didn't know then that I could go without it. Suddenly alcohol had made its mark on me. I was now depending on that drink.

New Farmers of America (NFA), 1953:
I was a freshman in high school when we began.

NFA, 1954: Our re-established group

NFA Boys: The two kneeling and me are the three
original members.

NFA Quintet in concert: Our high school reunion performance in 1988 after 30 Years apart. I am on the far right.

NFA Quartet: 1990

Chapter 5

MY FATHER'S DEATH

I believed—and a number of people had confirmed with their own sense of certainty—that if you had a car, you'd be sure to get a girlfriend. So I could hardly wait for my sixteenth birthday—April 12, 1953—when I could get a license allowing me to drive legally. Two weeks after my much-longed-for sixteenth birthday, I got my driver's permit. I was in paradise—drinking, smoking, working, shaving, and now, driving. Things were looking up.

Two weeks after receiving my permit, I found that trouble had come to paradise. I got my first speeding ticket. And there was no girl involved! I was carrying other guys to pick up their girls, but there was no girl for me. I was frustrated more than ever after being stopped by the police and getting the summons. Naturally, my drinking increased after that humiliation. Then it hit me. I was driving my father's pick-up truck. If I were driving a car, perhaps things would be different. So, I bought my first car, a 1950 Silver Streak Pontiac. It had been driven so hard by the previous owner that there wasn't much good left in it. I had to push it off the lot to get it started. It was a good-looking car, just no good for transportation.

I went to church every Sunday hoping to see Mabel, whom I had known since grade school. I drove her home after church sometimes. I smiled so much and spoke so little when I was with her. One day she asked me if I ever talked. I smiled and managed to get out what I thought was a cool, "Yeah, sometimes."

As soon as we reached her house, her father started clearing his throat—a clear sign for me to leave. That man frightened me, so I hauled my behind out of there. I thought about her all week. I lay on my bed or sat in a chair thinking of her smile, her words, her eyes. She had a great shape and was rather talkative. I could hardly wait for Sunday. But apparently her father—who always rolled his eyes upward when he cleared his throat—didn't drive everyone away. I was stunned and hurt to hear a conversation revealing that one of my football teammates had gotten her pregnant. That really hurt me, listening to two students in the hallway talk about her getting "knocked up, you know." What did I do? Drink! Drink! Drink!

I turned eighteen on April 12, 1955. My father died two weeks later. He was only fifty-two. Although Dad had been sick for a long time, he had refused to go to a doctor. He had health problems that could have been treated, but he wouldn't go to a hospital. He just wouldn't go unless his ailment was so severe he couldn't avoid it. That had happened in 1952 when he was carried to the hospital by ambulance. He had been flat on his back; writhing in pain for so long even he saw the necessity of getting to the hospital. He had congestive heart failure, a build-up of fluids around the lungs. Other than his epilepsy, that was the only ailment I remember; but there must have been more, because medical advisors said it was difficult prescribing medicine for Dad because medicine used for one ailment caused negative reactions for another one.

After he lost his eye, he started having spells. I now believe those seizures might have been associated with alcoholism. My father didn't drink regularly. I saw him drunk to excess only a couple times. He would crawl on his knees and cry.

"I won't do this again," he wailed.

When he drank, he went through a dramatic personality change. He slipped from a mood of depression to one of high-spirited talkativeness. He loved to talk and to keep people laughing. But no laughing audience could hide the fact that something was wrong with him. My father, once a six-foot, three-inch tall man weighing around 190 pounds, weighed only 128 pounds when he was last able to get on scales. Most of those pounds were just bones.

While he was sick, Dad had always wanted me around. I had to be around. Because of his illness and the loss of income, I had to work more to keep the family going. I drove a school bus in the morning, worked on the farm, and spent two days a week working at the sawmill. One morning Dad asked me to come right back home after my morning bus run.

"I came right back here yesterday," I reminded him.

"Yeah, I know, but come back today," he said, almost pleading.

I carried the kids to school and I was walking back home when I met Silas flying up the road on his bicycle. When he whizzed by me, he yelled: "Dad is dead," and kept pedaling toward town. Silas was sixteen and mean, but even he wouldn't play around like that, I thought. I looked at his figure disappearing up the road.   "Dad is dead." The words ricocheted in my head and I took off running. When I rushed, breathing heavily, through the front door, one look at my mother told me that Silas' message of death was true. I looked at my mother, her fingers on her face in despair, and I knew it was all over for Dad—and perhaps for us all.

"What happened?" I asked, almost choking.

"I don't know, Paul. It all happened so quickly and so quietly. I was making the bed and he rolled over to the other side of the bed like he always did while I tidied up his side. He tried to sit up, but just lay back—that was it. His heart just stopped."

I remembered telling Dad earlier that morning I was going to move when he died. Of course, I had no idea he was that ill, or that I was speaking to him on his deathbed. Maybe he had known he was dying and that's why he wanted me to come right back after taking the children to school. I hadn't thought about any of that then. A gust of anger pushed me on.

"I'm going to get the hell out of this place," I had said. "I don't want to be here and I'm going to leave."

I was just talking, venting some of my anger against my sisters and mother. The girls were having babies and Mom always took everything I had. I wasn't going to stay there so she and my sisters could use me. I would sell the animals and get on out.

I was angry with my father, too. He never really spoke up for himself. We were share farmers, and I saw how landowners treated him and I heard how they talked to him. They said that he was a thief. I wasn't going to take that mess. I had told him that when he died, I would be leaving. But I didn't know he was dying. I had just erupted like a volcano and everything just spewed out. It was a terrible thing to tell your father on the morning of his death.

To this day, I don't know what the coroner found when he performed an autopsy on Dad. Back then, people just didn't talk to children. I do know his heart was bad, his blood was drying up, and water was still on his lungs. With all of that, he also had a bad case of asthma. And he had prostate problems. Physically, he was beat.

The funeral director dressed Dad in a dark suit that I had bought for myself the Saturday before Dad died. I had gone to Sanford, North Carolina, and purchased it brand new for $49. I took it home, showed it to Dad, and he loved it. "This is beautiful," he said, "just what I would have chosen." Since we wore the same size and had the same taste in clothes, I knew I would bury him in that suit.

I didn't view the body before it was moved to the church. I just couldn't look at him, knowing it would be the last time I saw him. I was too fragile for that. My father had chosen me as the leader of the family. I viewed his body at the funeral.

"Son, the reason I ask you to do so much is because I know you can handle it," he had told me. "You can do so many things that will keep the family together."

I really did try to hold things together as best I could. While the rest of my family outwardly grieved to relieve their sadness, I had yet to shed a tear. I was telling them to take it easy, to be calm. I acted as if I were the role model by controlling my emotions. Although my grief took years to unravel, I was devastated when my father died. I felt alone in the world, without a friend. Dad was the only person who understood me, who never questioned me, and trusted me absolutely. When he died, my world collapsed.

I was in control right through the burial. I didn't break down. A tear might have slid down, but I stayed strong because I had to keep the family together. When we buried my father, I stayed at the cemetery until the grave was filled up and all other mourners had gone.

A bootlegger I went to see every weekend to buy corn liquor lived about a mile from the cemetery. I went to buy a quart of moonshine, and then went into the woods. I sat against a tree and tilted the bottle until liquor was half gone. Only then was I able to let my emotions go. I stood, pulled down three limbs from a tree and tore them into little pieces, one by one. I felt alone, but didn't want to be alone. I struck out at what was closest—a tree. I didn't feel drunk, but clearly I must have been;, a lost soul in the woods, screaming at and kicking at trees and breaking branches.

I came out of those woods feeling that my eyes— usually clear as crystal—were blood red and swollen. When I saw people in front of me as I walked home, I wiped my eyes as if there were something in them. Of course, that was just more of a form of denial, a cover-up—hiding my real feelings.

Once the rituals of death were over, it was crunch time for the family, and especially for me since I was left in charge. Dad had made all the decisions about what to do, when to do it, and how much to do about the farm. Well, he was gone now. My mother didn't have too much experience about managing a farm—at least, I thought she didn't. Everything fell in my lap. I was stuck now with running the farmstead. I still drove the school bus and still worked at the sawmill. I had to keep those last two jobs. But I made up my mind that we were going to quit farming. The landowners made me sick.

We were working for Luke Marin then. I told my mother that as soon as we sold our crop and settled our debt with him, we would be through with farming. And when our tobacco crop came in, that's what we did. We also had some farm animals—two hogs, two mules, a cow, and some chickens. I sold them for just a little of nothing, just change almost. Why not? I had quit farming.

We rented a small shack for twelve dollars a month. I thought we could afford that. Even though things were a lot cheaper then, it must be remembered that wages, too, were paid on the cheap. The point is, finally we had broken from the farm.

I had told my father we would do that, and we did. I had also told him I would avenge his poor treatment. He was not really accepted by a lot of his relatives—they were all halves, anyway. Their rejection had a lot to do with the anger and hostility I had toward some of my cousins and other people. After his death, I sought out some of the men who I knew had hurt him and I picked fights with them and beat them all. It was a hostile thing to do, but that's where I was at the time. Having done two of the things I had promised Dad, I aimlessly continued working and going to school.

At this time Juanita Mae Maness walked into my life. She was a shy one. Her father was deceased, but her mother was very much alive and had put the fear of God in me. Juanita's sisters and brothers didn't seem to like me, either. When I went to see her, which was every night, I felt I had to strengthen myself with a drink. We courted for about two years. She played games with my head by dating other guys, too. I tried to play it off with a smile, but it hurt me a lot. I was afraid if I showed how I really felt, she would quit me. I suppressed my feelings as best I could. With the emptiness and loneliness came more drinking.

Four other fellows rode with me as my partners. We drank all the time, especially on weekends, and we started a lot of trouble. We stole goats, geese, gas, and everything else we could to support our drinking. We even picked up dead rabbits from the side of the road and traded them for booze. One Sunday, we rode over to my girl's house and saw three boys from another town sitting on the front porch. I always carried my twelve-gauge shotgun in my car, and I had no reservations about shooting it. After seeing these guys, we turned around and waited for them to leave. My partners wanted to beat them up, but I had other ideas. When the unwelcome visitors came out to the porch, I aimed my shotgun and put a hole in the side of their car. We never saw them again.

Two years after my father died, I graduated from high school. Most kids my age had graduated two years earlier. I was lucky to get out at all. Shortly before graduating, I had fired my shotgun into the back door of the school's gymnasium. I was aiming at some basketball players who had started a fight and tried beating us up. I had also turned over two cars and wrecked an activity bus with thirty-two football players on it. One player was injured, as well as the man in the car. He later died as a result of the accident. After all of this activity, I was lucky to be alive, better yet, graduating. And then, two months after I graduated, Juanita and I were married.

On a Saturday morning in August, a justice of the peace performed our marriage ceremony. After we had tied the knot, I didn't know how to behave, so I did what I always did when frustrated—went out and got drunk. I was drunk for two days. After I sobered up, I went to Port Chester, New York.

The Northernaires, a popular gospel singing quintet at the time, wanted me to join them. They featured titles like

"I Love To Call My Saviour's Name," "One Day When The Lord Shall Call Me," "Go Down Moses," and "Oh Let Us Go Back To Our Fathers Praying Ground." I would bass deeply on the lyrics, "Oh Let us go back....come on....come on...come on...."

The group contacted me through my sister. "You guys are going to be famous and rich," she promised. "Just wait and see." So I, Paul A. Austin, who had hardly been out of my backyard, headed for New York. I didn't worry about who was going to take care of my mother or my wife. I just wanted to get away; that's all I had on my mind. I got a job as a porter at United Hospital in Portchester, New York. Six weeks later I went back to North Carolina and picked up my wife. We found a room in Rye, New York, less than an hour from Harlem.

We wouldn't be in that one room long. I believed, like my sister, that once "discovered" in New York, I would quickly become a millionaire, or at least someone with a whole lot of prestige. That was my first "geographical cure." Without having worked through any of my problems, I was simply going to move to the bright lights of the big city—and things were going to be different. I was going to make my mark.

Actually, New York was too fast for me. I lasted five years doing real well as if I were going up the ladder. No sooner than I was up, I came down, brought low by alcoholism. It brought me to my knees. I was going up and down like a yo-yo.

Shortly after I arrived in New York, I met with The Northernaires. They wanted me to sing bass for them. After I was introduced to the group, we went to a lounge. They ordered screwdrivers, which sounded like Kool-Aid to me, so I ordered a half-pint. Everyone looked at me as if to say, "What the hell is he doing?" I had never been inside a fancy bar before and had no idea of how to conduct myself. I began to sweat really bad. After I a few doubles, I thought I would 'fess up.

"This is the first time I have been in a bar," I said sheepishly. They would have understood at the outset if I had only admitted it. I just couldn't.

I joined the group officially, and once we began to sing, we traveled a lot. We bought new, stylish suits. I thought I looked good, but boy was I afraid. I eventually bought a pink Lincoln with a beige top. I sent pictures of my Lincoln and me back to North Carolina so the folk I had left behind could see how well I was doing. My mother thought it was great.

When my first child was born in the United Hospital in Port Chester, New York, on September 12, 1958, I was a wreck. My wife was in labor for 12 hours. When I could stand it no longer, I went to the liquor store and bought a pint of Four Roses. From a nearby drug store, I bought a box of cigars that said, "It's a Boy!" My wife was still in labor. I often wonder, "what if it had been a girl?" I passed out cigars to anybody I met in the hospital. They congratulated me on a son that was not yet here. It was a boy, weighing in at 7 pounds, 15 ounces, and 19 inches long.

This was the beginning of a family that was preoccupied by many, many fears. We were a family started by two people who didn't even know themselves, much less anything about life and the meaning of it. I got another job driving a trash truck and making seventy-five dollars a week to supplement my income from the quartet. My wife didn't work; she hardly left the house. My singing engagements increased and I met people in all walks of life. I even met Ed Sullivan's sister, who told me if I stopped drinking, she would get me on her brother's television show, the most popular variety show on network television. She took me into New York City once to meet some television executives. She had asked me not to drink when we arrived in the Manhattan. I was so uptight. I told myself that I needed a drink. We went into one of those up-scale cocktail lounges where I knew I didn't belong. She ordered dinner for us, but I just had to have one drink. Of course, I had three or four and started to run my mouth, talking nonsense and slurring my words. They watched me with odd expressions, almost as if they felt sorry for me. That was my first, and last, trip into the city with her.

Dad died here: My dad passed in this house on April 28, 1955. I had just turned 18 on April 12.

Last farm: We had our last farm here; after this last year of farming, I sold everything, including the animals. Two years later at age 20, I married and left North Carolina to start my singing career.

Moore County Court House, Carthage, NC: I was married in the court house in 1957 at a cost of $3.00. Three days later, I left for New York for my singing career. Over the years my alcoholism progressed. I was locked up many, many, many times here when I would visit my home. In 1971, I was chained up, and a judge made me sign my rights away to never return. I never returned again until I was sober, many years later.

The Northernairs: I was 21 when this was taken in 1958.

Chapter 6

SINGING ZION'S SONGS AND DRINKING HELL'S FIRE

I worked diligently at the church my sister attended in Mt. Vernon, New York. I sang in the choir and helped raise collection. I was good at getting other people's money—a trait the pastor noticed and loved. Many church members thought I was the nicest fellow who was definitely going places. There was even talk of making me a junior deacon.

"This church needs some young blood," I heard.

I had to "join" the church, not just work in it. Joining meant baptism, a religious requirement in the Baptist Church that I had never experienced. I didn't want any fingers full of water sprinkling drops on my head. I would have to be dipped beneath the water. The thought of being dipped, rather than dripped, terrified me. I, who couldn't swim, imagined headlines:

Local Singer Drowns in Baptismal Pool

Pride, rather than faith, kept me from turning back. So I went through the baptism praying I wouldn't drown.

As the congregation sang "Take Me to the Water to Be Baptized," fear gripped me. The pastor put his hand around my waist, mumbled something about salvation, and before I realized what had happened, propelled me beneath the water—back first. I was totally unprepared. Water poured into my open mouth and down my throat. I felt as if I were strangled. When they brought me up, I knew this wouldn't work a second time. If I had to repeat this ordeal, certainly, I would drown—and they're always repeating rituals in the church.

I was baptized, but not sanctified, and saved only to bolt from the church. I didn't go right away, but while there I listened for announcements of repeat baptisms.

Juanita became pregnant with our second child and I applied for a job as an electrical zinc plate operator at Rushell, Burtschell and Ward Bolt and Nut Factory. I got the job, but my progressive alcoholism caused me to miss many days at work. Since I still looked respectable and could get drunk and then sober up quickly, I ignored the signals that my increased drinking were sending, and missed days at work. Eventually, I lost the job.

I still sang with the Northernaires, and we made tours to North Carolina, Virginia, Massachusetts, Connecticut, and New Jersey. Our popularity got us featured on local radio stations—and even on television. We'd meet people and they would say, "Look who's come to town!"

Some weekends, I binged and hung out in clubs with Brook Benton and Joe Henderson (the one who made the song, "Snap Your Fingers"). Invariably, the gospel group found out about my antics and wouldn't allow me to sing with them.

I sang with the Northernaires for five years until my alcoholism dropped me lower in their eyes than even my bass voice could support. They wanted me out. I drank heavily on Friday and Saturday nights and would be wrestling with a hangover on Sundays, the day of our concerts. I was so sick one Sunday morning I could hardly move. Yet, I was scheduled to leave town to sing.

I called Harvey to tell him that I couldn't make it. "My car has broken down," I explained lamely.

"Can you drive it at all?"

"Naw, man! It's got a bad-sounding knock in the engine." You damn right it had a knock. I had wired a bolt to the fan, and when the fan turned, the bolt hit certain parts of the car.

"Well, don't worry, we'll be right over to pick you up." His voice trailed off and then there was silence.

Oh God, I had to keep these people from coming over. I was in no condition to sing. Before long, they were there to pick me up. I had to find a way out of this thing. I just had to. Before I could say or do anything, I heard:

"Crank her up . . ." It was Roy Williams. " . . . so I can hear that noise you talking about."

At that moment I knew they hadn't believed my story. I cranked the Lincoln—and *bam, bam, bam.* "Knocking just like I told you!" I said.

Roy didn't let it go. "Raise the hood and I'll take a look."

That's when it all came out. I refused to open the hood to let them see what I had done. From then on, our singing together became erratic, primarily because of my drinking. The guitar player in the group had an alcohol problem as well. We drank together and we drank hard. Finally, the other guys who were pretty stable, and who had stopped their drinking years ago, wanted to perform without us. They had enough and didn't want to put up with us. Plus, our drinking was giving the group a bad reputation. Many people in our audiences were obviously embarrassed by the tipsy behavior of the guitar player and me, and they began to look at us funny.

The group broke up. Roy became an evangelist, even though he performed some music "out in the world." Cecil Brownley organized his own group. George, the guitar player, went to play for another group and he stopped drinking without going for treatment. He just stopped; moved to Long Island, away from the Westchester area and away from me. He's been free from alcohol for more than four decades.

Only James and I remained in the area, so we formed a new group, The Sensational Versatones. James, Tony, Don, and I made up this quartet. All of us had good voices, but I could switch from bass to baritone. When there was not a bass song featured, I sang baritone. The quartet consisted first of second tenors, baritone, and a lead singer. It was a good group, but no matter, our talent or our name; my problem remained.

The group knew about my illness when we organized. They felt that they could handle the problem. Their first line of defense was to watch me. Next, they mixed my drinks. They wanted to ride me; they wanted to lend me their cars. They bought me scotch and milk which they called the "no-problem person's drink." I wanted Italian Swiss Colony Port or Old Crow. They were so occupied with watching me that it became frustrating not only to me, but also to them. It wasn't long before this group, too, broke up.

James Ruffins died in December 1977. The Northernaires were invited to the funeral, but I didn't go. I hadn't been out of treatment long enough (1974) to risk it.

The breakup of the Sensational Versatones occurred around the birth of my fourth child—February 15, 1963. I had no group, no job, and my family was put out in the street—again. We were also put out after the birth of our third child. I went from place to place trying to survive and to find food for my family. I went to meat markets and begged for the scraps the butcher threw away after trimming a cut of meat. I would ask if I could look at meat scraps for my dog. One butcher said to me: "I notice you don't get nothing but the lean. Don't your dog like any fat meat?" That made me hot. I left the meat markets alone and started stealing chickens. Some people had their own little chicken yards back then.

With the birth of our fourth child, I ventured into new territory. I fiddled around with welfare. I received $246 a month with which I was to pay rent and buy food for the six of us. With my first check, I took some of the money and bought a nice truck. Unfortunately, I tore it to pieces before it was registered or had license plates on it. I totaled it on a New York City parkway. So now I had no truck, but enough welfare money to get us situated. The welfare people told our new landlord to put the family out if I failed to pay the rent.

I was still on welfare when our fifth child was born. While Juanita was in the hospital, I spent the rent money. I knew the landlord would put me out, because he had already said he would. I had to do something, and it had to be done quickly. After much thought, I figured I would set the house on fire, stay in the burning apartment until the firemen came, then I'd jump from the burning building, perhaps breaking an arm or leg. In my drunken stupor, it looked like a great plan. First, after the house burned down, I wouldn't have to pay the rent that I didn't have. Second, I might get a lot of sympathy from well-wishers and do-gooders who wanted to help this poor father who had lost everything, including his life. It was perfect. I might even get an increase in my welfare payment and be on television for all to see. The money would roll in.

I had to do something with the children, though. I took them to relatives to look after them during the day until Juanita came home from the hospital. I was supposed to look after the children during the night.

On the night of the fire, I undressed down to my shorts to make it appear as if I had been lying on the sofa asleep when the fire broke out. Undressed, I torched the place and waited for someone to call the fire department. Smoke filled the apartment, wood cracked as flames swept over it. I waited, hoping the fire trucks would arrive soon. I didn't want to jump before they arrived, but it was getting hot in there. I wanted the firemen to see me take my leap so they could corroborate that the fire wasn't a hoax. By the time the firemen did arrive, flames had devoured the downstairs steps. Just as the fire truck pulled up in the driveway, I jumped. There were no broken bones, just bruises. The firemen put a fire jacket and boots on me and carried me to a fire truck.

Other firemen were in the building with axes cutting the house up. They threw out an old TV and I thought: "Throw everything out, don't save nothing." When they finally finished, the firemen drove me up to the fire station and told me that I could get out.

"Get out! Ain't you gone do nothing for me?" I asked. "I almost got burned up and most definitely got burned out, and now you're turning me out."

"We did all we could do; we put the fire out," one of them said.

"But, don't you help people who get burned out to get back on their feet?"

"Yes we do, but not for you. We can look at your face and tell you are not one of the people we usually help."

What did they see on my face? Alcohol? Poverty? Deception? Blackness? I never figured that out. I just went to the thrift shop and got some clothes and shoes. I got no help from anybody. My wife's relatives came up from Washington, DC, picked up my family and took them to DC until I got back on my feet.

I vowed to get a new job, a new life, and a new apartment. In the meantime, my sister was paying my rent at a fleabag hotel. One day, I got a letter at this hotel. I was scared to open it; maybe they'd found out I set the fire. I didn't open the letter for two or three days. Finally, when I did, I found a check for $280 from the IRS. They said that an error had been made—to my advantage.

Old habits die hard. Just as I had taken part of my first welfare check and bought a truck, I took $250 of this money and bought a 1955 Chrysler Imperial. Somehow or another, I got plates on it. The next thing I did was to move from my fleabag hotel. What I didn't do was stop drinking.

I'm a night owl. One night while drinking and driving, I blacked out and almost ran over a policeman—a street guard or somebody like that. I came to consciousness in a parking lot where a couple of police cars surrounded me.

"Paul, if this happens again, or if anything else happens to you, we're going to send you to Valhalla."

That's where the state nuthouse was. A week later, they reversed themselves and told me to leave the state of New York. That hurt me and it hurt badly.

I bought a pint of Four Roses, drank it, and everything seemed clear. I would get my behind out of New York. Without a second thought about it, I got on the highway and headed south. Somewhere along the way, I stopped and got another pint of booze. A New Jersey State Highway patrol officer stopped me way down on the New Jersey Turnpike. He asked for my license and registration. He took them, then asked me to follow him.

I had an opened pint bottle of booze on the front seat. I was afraid to move it. If I reached over to scoot it somewhere, the officer might think I was searching for a gun. He probably would have shot me. I left the half-empty pint bottle right there on the seat.

I followed the highway patrol officer about ten miles to a Howard Johnson's on the turnpike. We pulled in, he parked, and told me to park my car and lock it up. Out of luck again! Jail, I thought, and I had no money for bail. As I locked the door, I managed to slide the booze under the seat. I followed the officer into Howard Johnson's where he took my keys. The officer gave my keys and license to one of the waitresses and told her to give them back to me in an hour, after I'd had as much black coffee as I wanted.

I sat there and talked a lot of junk and drank coffee for an hour. By this time, I had it made. I mean, I established a good relationship with the waitress and started to lie. I told her that I knew the highway patrol officer who stopped me because we worked together as highway patrol officers. When the hour was up, she gave me my license and keys. We had struck up such a good relationship; I stayed on for another hour.

When I left New Jersey, passed through Delaware and crossed into Maryland, I felt sad and empty. Leaving New York against my will really shook me up. Maybe it was for the best. I missed my family and was headed for Washington to see my children. Right there on the highway, I resolved that when this journey ended, I was going to clean up my act.

When I got into Washington, I went directly to my in-laws' house. I ached to see Juanita and the children. They were flabbergasted to see me—more disappointed than excited. I believe they thought they had gotten rid of me.

There I was smiling to beat the band to see them and they were standing there as if to say, "Here he is again." Juanita took me inside and started asking questions. She wondered where was I going to stay and what was I going to do. I wound up staying with them at my in-laws.

Once in DC, I needed to find out where people like me hung out. I found places like 14th Street, NW; Fairmont Heights; and Seat Pleasant, Maryland. You could find the bums, thugs, and any other social outcast you wanted to find in these areas. I didn't necessarily want to join them, but they appeared to be the only people in the city who accepted me.

I found them all right, and soon found that I was getting locked up on a consistent basis. I also found out about the art of panhandling. For example, when asking for money on the streets, you never ask for even money, always uneven—23 cents, 51 cents, 47 cents. This leads the giver to think that you already have some money and are just trying to make up enough.

The longer I stayed in the DC-Maryland area, the lower I sank. I had gotten so bad I lay down in front of a transit bus and refused to move until the driver paid me $1.50. At that time, with seventy-five cents you could buy a bottle of wine; with thirty-two cents a pack of Pall Mall cigarettes. That left me with a few pennies to begin my daily panhandling.

One day I dressed up like a bum and took my oldest sons, Ivan and Paul, panhandling with me. They held a can that I had put a few pennies in and shook it when people passed, asking them to help the blind. I wore a pair of extra dark sunglasses. My sons—just eight and ten years old—had shame and hurt written all over their young faces.

My in-laws didn't care for me because of what they felt I had done to Juanita and the children who were now living with me in DC. They had gotten me arrested once when I tried to barge into their Maryland home uninvited and flashed a straight razor. The police locked me up. When I came before a judge, no one testified against me. The judge kept me in court all day hoping someone would come to testify against me.

"If they do, I'm giving your behind ten years," he told me.

No one came. The judge let me go, but not before advising me to leave Maryland and not return. "If I see or hear of you in one of my courts, you're getting 10 years just for being in Maryland."

I moved to DC. For six months I tried to control my drinking, but in the end went back to my old ways. For the first time in our marriage, Juanita left me and moved in with her mother and sister. Of course, she took the children with her. I begged her to return home—where we were threatened with eviction. But she stayed where she was.

By this time, I was drinking heavily and feeling a great pain. One night I decided to end it all. In my mind, that didn't mean suicide, but killing my wife. I figured I wouldn't get more than twenty years for murder and would be out of jail when I was only forty-eight years old. I spent the rest of that night sharpening my knife.

The following morning, I went to the liquor store on the corner of Division and Grant Streets and bought two half pints of Canada Dry Liquor—cheap stuff. I drank one half-pint straight down, went back home and drank half of the other pint. I figured it would be a long time before I'd get another drink. I put on my long coat and headed for my mother-in-law's house in DC. I sneaked in behind the hedges and in seconds had kicked down both doors and was inside swinging my knife. The women and children were running.

Juanita tried to calm things down. "I'll go back with him. I can talk to him," she told her family.

She walked toward me and looked in my eyes. I planned to stab her in the chest when she got close enough. When I raised the knife, she threw up her arm and the blade went through her arm. Blood flew everywhere—even on me. When the police burst into the house, they thought I was the victim so much blood was on me. When they found out I was the one who wielded the knife, they beat the hell out of me before putting me in chains.

I was arraigned the next day. The whole family was there; some wrapped in bandages and others just looking hurt. The judge gave me four years but put me on probation for two, demanding that I "stop drinking and stop carrying a knife." I promised never to drink again, but I kept my knife.

Chapter 7

DON'T GO THERE

I finally went into Coral Hills, Maryland, and signed up to be a bus driver. By this time, all my hair was out. It just fell out. So I wore a loose hat pulled way down to my ears. People must have thought I was crazy. After the training, I was to be bareheaded and wear dark pants and a white shirt. I didn't have any clothes. I told the bus trainer I couldn't go bareheaded. He said that would be okay and told the company supervisor that he was in danger of losing a good man because he refused to go bareheaded. One of the supervisors walked up to me one day and asked, "If we let you wear a bus uniform hat, will you stay?"

"Okay, I will do that," I said. I was a good worker, showing up on time and being diligent and dependable. In six months, I was a training supervisor.

Soon I was driving the sightseeing tours. I was also taking the bus company money to the bank. Everyone trusted me so much. I was an impressive young man with ability, who didn't drink, and knew where he was going in life.

People at the uptown terminals and other places where I drove said that I looked as if I had stepped off a page of *Esquire* magazine. I was so clean. I wore my uniform, my D.J. Kaufman suits, with everything matching. I was a perfectionist, really, kind of an extremist—no gray, only all white or black. That's who I was.

For the next two years I didn't drink. But I watched the others drink. They held their liquor in those small paper cups—Lily Cups—and didn't act the way I did when I drank. Suddenly this seemed to be the answer to my drinking problem—use Lily Cups. If I ever drank again, it would be that way.

But watching other people drink was a fascinating experience that made me real curious. I was getting this readout in my mind that I had not fully learned how to drink. Maybe if I learned how to drink properly, I could be a successful, comfortable drinker. I told myself that if I ever drank again, I would drink out of Lily Cups. I had seen people drinking out of Lily Cups. It was so neat how they put their mixes in it, read the papers, talked to one another in the parking lot or went about their business. And they were pouring their booze out of half gallons and fifths—pouring it into Lily Cups.

I said to myself, "You know there's got to be something to this." By now I was at the point of shaking uncontrollably after coming off a drunk. I didn't realize that I was suffering from a physical allergy and an obsession of the mind. So I watched carefully those people who drank out of the Lily Cups, especially early in the mornings. I wanted to see their eyes, to see if their cornea were red, to see if they were tipping around, to see if they were shaking. I always had the shakes. But, they didn't appear to be shaking! They appeared to be always out front, going on with their work and stuff. I was totally convinced after this review of their conduct that if I drank out of Lily Cups, I would be a total success.

After two years, I knew the day would come when the frustration and the pain of being at the top and wondering where I go from here would overwhelm me and cause me to drink again. But, at least I would be a prosperous drinker because I would be drinking out of Lily Cups.

Had I been a wise drunk, I would have been able to get a lot of booze for free on April 4, 1968, because that was the day Martin Luther King was assassinated. When the riots broke out in DC, people were actually trying to give me cases of booze. I rejected and refused in an aggressive way. "Get away from me, get out of my face. I don't drink—get out of my face." Had I known that I would be back drinking, I would have collected those cases and been well on my way.

My drink out of the Lily cup came about April 18. Harley and Frank, two bus drivers, were with me.

"I'm going to take a drink, too," I said. I was looking for their response. The guilt was churning inside me although I hadn't had a drink yet. My voice and everything changed. I could just feel it.

Harley looked at me strangely and said, "Paul, you don't drink."

I said, "Sure I drink."

"Well, we've been around you for two years, and we've never seen you take a drink," said Frank.

I said, "I've been too busy, and I haven't really had time to drink." This was the denial phase of my illness— alcoholism. My defensiveness was coming out.

Harley spoke up: "If you haven't drank in two years, why are you going to drink now?"

"Stop meddling in my business, and get the hell out of my face," I told him. That was the aggression already coming out before the alcohol had even gotten in me. So I asked Frank if he would go into the liquor store down in Coral Hills. I was too paranoid to be seen by anybody because they might think I was going to drink. I told Frank to buy a fifth, and I named the brand that was on sale that week. "And don't forget the Lily Cups." This was of great importance. "Hey," I said, "bring a little can of Donald Duck grapefruit juice, unsweetened."

He bought the fifth, the Lily Cups, and the grapefruit juice, and we went out behind the Plain and Fancy Donut Shop in Coral Hills. We sat on the cement steps that led to the kitchen. I opened the fifth and the box of Lily Cups, and I poured a big shot into the Lily Cup. Then I pulled the tab off the grapefruit juice can. I was getting ready to drink, and I was nervous. I drank some Donald Duck grapefruit juice behind it, and I passed the bottle to Harley and said, "You see there, I just was going to take a drink; that's all I wanted, one drink. Here, you can have the bottle." So I gave him the bottle, the Lily Cups, and the grapefruit juice, and they just stood there and stared at me as if something strange was about to happen.

And, sure enough, it did. Within 15 minutes after I had stood up, all hell broke loose. My eyes were jumping, my teeth were gritting. Harley was holding the bottle. "Give me my bottle back; I bought it." He looked at me strangely, then passed it back to me. I started to drink as I remembered drinking before I gave it up two years earlier.

I understand today that if you start to drink after some elapsed time, you don't start where you are, you start back where you would have been if you had continued drinking throughout the period. That's the progression. I drank that bottle, mostly by myself, and I bought two more fifths before I left Plain and Fancy Donuts. I helped drink them all.

I began to experience strange physical changes. My face felt tight, my voice cracked, and I kept blinking my eyes. Then Harley went to the top of the hill leading from the donut shop and began to pass the word on to the other drivers up there that Paul Austin was behind Plain and Fancy Donuts, and he's taken a drink, you ought to see him. People began to line up as if there were accident or funeral parade. They came down there one by one—standing, watching me, looking.

Several went back with, "Paul Austin is drinking, and he's acting strange." They went upstairs to the bus company president and told him, "Your training supervisor is behind Plain and Fancy Donut Shop drinking."

I stayed there and got drunk.

One of the ways I know today that I was out of control was that during the time that I had stopped for two years, I wouldn't wet my pants. Now I stood right there, outside, in the parking lot, behind the donut shop, with a clean uniform on, and peed in my uniform. It was wet all down the front.

I don't know what happened when I left. I know I didn't run my bus route. I went in to a blackout. When I came to, I was at Alfred's house. He was throwing a party. He was one of the guys who wanted my job badly. He had been envious because I was the training supervisor instead of him. Everybody was giving me everything—all of the whiskey and beer I wanted to drink for free.

I came out of the blackout the next morning. Alfred had gone earlier to the head of the company to tell him that I had been drunk all night and had been at his house, and had drunk up all of his liquor and beer. This was a set-up. When I came in, I was told to go up to the office. They sat me down. Mr. Miller, the head, looked at me as if he knew something was going on.

"I heard you were drinking last night; is that true?" he asked.

"Yes."

He said, "Paul, you can't drink and be training supervisor because the boys won't respect you. I'll have to take you off training if you drink."

"Mister Miller, I promise you from the bottom of my heart, that I won't drink and drive," I said. "Last night was just a mistake; it won't happen again."

I was trembling. I left the room to go out to train. I could see a lot of people looking out of the corner of their eyes. I was feeling really paranoid. I felt dirty, I felt guilty, and I felt remorseful. I was on a hangover. I couldn't imagine those other fellows who drank out of the Lily Cups feeling like that.

About 3 p.m., while driving the training bus, I began to tremble badly. "Look, I'm going to make sure you all pass your tests for bus drivers when the thing's over, but I just got to get me some beer," I told them. We stopped the bus and I got a six-pack. I was drinking and shaking in the back of the bus, and naturally they got lost.

When I parked the bus that evening, people at the company and the drivers too, were staring at me. I felt trapped as I drove away in my car. I told myself that I was not going to drink. But I couldn't help it; I had to drink. I went back to the liquor store and bought six more Schlitz beers, and I drove about 10 miles out in the country, back in the woods so nobody could see me. I felt hidden and protected. I drank the beer and looked around as if I were a thief hiding out. "I'm going to drink this six-pack and that's going to be it," I said to myself. But I was just pouring gas on the fire because a compulsion came over me that didn't die for four years.

♦

The only time I didn't drink in the next four years was when I was locked up, in Detox, in the hospital or so hurt that I just couldn't get alcohol. But I continued to drink, and a month after those six Schlitz beers, I was fired—no job. Next, I totaled my car. Soon I was at a place I had never been before in my life—skid row. For years I slept in empty houses and parked cars. I ate out of garbage cans. I broke both legs. I was always into something— trouble, DTs, the whole bit. I didn't want to be this way, but I had no choice. I was in pain and didn't know what to do. The bus company had fired me and this seemed like the end of my life.

I had the feeling that this had been my bus company. Oscar, an operator whom I had taught to drive, was finishing his training for the company. Boy, this really got my goat. I planned to hurt him because I felt he was to blame for all of my failures. And I would hang around the company and beg nickels and dimes to get a drink. I could see the hurt in their eyes because of what had happened to me. I had a little money in the bank on the hill near the bus company. But I was afraid to take it out because I felt that the people in the bank would think I was coming to hold up the bank. I felt that everyone was watching me and talking about me. I was drunk every day. I would be out before the sun came up so no one would see me. My personal hygiene had gone fast—no baths, no haircuts, and no shaves. My eyes stayed red, and I had the look of a crazy man. People would see me coming and leave, afraid of what would happen.

I got picked up by the police and taken to the DC Detox that had opened five years earlier. It had about 75 beds. I was in for a 72-hour detoxification. As soon as I got released, I would head for the alcohol. I believed that I had to have it to live.

I huddled with my buddies around fire barrels, eating from cans we cooked in. We got old meat and vegetables that they hadn't sold from the Florida Avenue Farmers Market dumpsters. We had the strangest conversations during those gatherings of skid row bums. We talked about how alcohol kills all germs. We even talked about how not to get drunk. "Eat butter, raw eggs, and clams on the half shell," was one suggestion. Yeah, I thought, if I had money for those items, I could buy enough Wild Irish Rose to last me for months. We also drank 200 percent grain alcohol and orange juice; and we mixed paint thinner in water. It's called smoke and will blow your mouth off if you smoke a cigarette at the same time. But the good thing about smoke is that it would stop the shakes. Sometimes during this period, I would be charged for being drunk and disorderly and faced a judge. But my drinking was never mentioned in these court appearances.

On June 10, 1969, I was shot in the stomach by a policeman at 44th and Dean Avenue in Washington, DC. I had attacked the policeman and tried to take his gun. I was carried to DC General Hospital where they would operate. I had ten holes in my intestines and two holes in my stomach. The bullet was lodged in my back near the spine, where it would stay for over seven years before it moved. As I lay in the intensive care unit, I hoped I would die. But God wouldn't have it that way. I came out of the hospital in 10 days and before the stitches were all out, I was drinking Wild Irish Rose wine. The *Washington Post* had reported that I was killed.

My wife let me come home to convalesce. As soon as she went to work and the kids were all in school, my drinking bums would come over to drink, and they would steal anything that was worth stealing.

An old drinking friend stopped by one day to see how I was doing. She told me that two men were following and bothering her. She wanted me to cut them for her. I told her for a drink I would do the job if she could get them close enough where I wouldn't hurt myself, because of the operation I had had. She arranged for me to get close. When they saw the shape I was in, they knew I was no trouble, and would be less if I were drunk. So, they bought me some booze and beer. When I drank it, she asked me when was I going to cut them. I told her if she didn't get the hell out of my face, I would cut her, because those guys had bought me booze and were now my friends.

Alcohol is cunning and powerful, and it brings with it many attitudes and personalities. Three months later, I was a recipient of the welfare system.

I really upset that office badly when I went to get my official eligibility for welfare. I stopped 18 people from work as I insisted that I didn't want anybody to mess up. When I walked toward the exit, I had food stamps, tokens, and a check in my pocket. Just as I was going out the door, I warned them that if one check should ever be late, I would come back and really make a disturbance.

"Does everybody understand me?" I asked as I left.

I used the money each month to buy booze. I would buy food, and when the money would run out, I would sell the meat to buy more booze. Some people thought I was running a meat market.

It wasn't long before my wife went to welfare and told them what I was doing and had the check changed to her name. When I didn't get a check, I went to find out what happened, then got drunk, went into a blackout, and assaulted my wife. I tore up the house and got locked up. I was back on the jail circuit.

I was in and out of jail—mostly Detox. When I was arrested, the police would chain me up for fear of what I would do. Once I stole a 38 pistol from a man and pawned it for booze. When I would get money, I would pick it up again, and then repawn it.

One of my hangouts was the bus company. The owner, W.W. Miller, would give me as much as one hundred dollars to get me away. He really liked me, but didn't understand what had happened to me and was very hurt about my condition. He would tell me to go and spend it wisely. He would also call the Washington, DC, and Maryland police, and tell them not to arrest me unless I started trouble.

One day I had drunk two fifths of Wild Irish Rose wine and climbed onto the building of the bus company. I staged an ambush and tried to jump onto Alfred's head. I missed, breaking my left ankle and heel. I was taken to the hospital by ambulance. They X-rayed me and put a cast on. By midnight, I had it off. I needed alcohol and couldn't get to it with a cast on my foot. So I removed the casts.

By this time, I was having DTs and seizures, and I was carried to the hospital by ambulance on a regular basis. When the emergency room was notified it was me, they would just say, "It's him again," meaning Paul Austin. That would really hurt. Nobody wanted me anymore. The man with many talents and great promise had fallen prey to the dogs. God, there seemed no way out—I couldn't kill myself, and no one else had done the job either. Where would it end—the shame and embarrassment I had brought on myself and all others who had loved me so much at one time? How could I go on facing the dark days ahead? God only knew.

In 1971, one of my brothers, a skid row bum, died in Washington, DC. I was unable to attend the funeral because I had nothing to wear, and I also had a jammed hip because I had tried to kick down the door to my wife's apartment.

Soon I began to run from city to city and state to state, not being accepted anyplace, being locked up at every stop. In 1971, I jumped bond in Washington, DC, after being released from jail, and went to Carthage, North Carolina. It was late April. When I arrived I was paranoid. Everybody in North Carolina looked at me very strangely and moved away from me. By the time the police picked me up in June, I had already been arrested four times for being drunk and disorderly. I had also gotten a broken leg.

Florence was an old girlfriend from high school who had been married for about 20 years. But my alcohol told me that she was still mine. When I arrived at her house on a Saturday morning to see her, her husband met me at the door and asked me to leave. I refused. He pushed me off his porch, and when I fell, I broke my leg. The police then took me to jail.

I stayed locked up until Sunday afternoon, when a bondsman came to get me out. He had a half-gallon of homemade wine in his car. I needed a drink badly, but I thought if I drink with him he would just get me locked up again. What the hell, I drank anyway. If I was to be locked up, it would be better if I were drunk.

On Monday evening, my sister took me to Pinehurst Hospital in Moore County. They took X-rays and told me I had a broken fibula in my right leg. They put a cast on. Meantime, I already had an artificial bone in my left foot. That foot is a whole inch shorter than the right one, and that had put a lot of pressure on my left foot and leg.

One week later, the U.S. Marshals arrived from DC. They had called the North Carolina police a week earlier. Just before they arrived, I had gone to church and upset the whole congregation with my wild, alcoholic bantering. My mother and sister had to take me out, looking over their shoulders with embarrassment and shame. On June 1, the North Carolina police arrested me and took me to jail for holding until the marshals arrived to extradite me.

At Carthage Court House, I faced a judge who had an order for me to sign for extradition, waiving my rights to remain there in Carthage. The order stated I must never come to Carthage again. I was a fugitive from justice.

I was chained up again. This time it was with two other men, one wanted for murder, and the other for kidnapping and rape. We were on the road for 11 days. They had us in lineups all along the way, to see if anyone else wanted us for anything, as we passed coming back.

When we arrived in Washington, DC, in 1971, and entered the U.S. Court House, I was placed on a $40,000 bond. I spent the whole summer in jail. I was carried to court from jail 19 times that summer to face trial. I faced five judges and a grand jury before they let me go. When I was turned loose in September 1971, I had no place to go and no one to contact. I went to the mission on Fifth and G Streets, NW, and asked if I could stay there.

"Can you sing and pray?" they asked.

I said, "Sure!"

During the entire time I was locked up, I kept saying to myself, "I'll never drink again." But the minute I got out, this commitment changed. I thought one beer won't hurt. So I got myself a beer and a white potato. I drank the beer and ate the potato and went into the mission to begin the night services. Boy, did I sing and pray! I was so glad to be out of jail.

The next morning, I asked a DC Transit bus driver if I could ride to Deanwood with him, and told him that I had no money. He said, "Yes, but go in the back of the bus where other people won't be near you." Deanwood was where my old drinking buddies were. This is where I had been on skid row before, and it was starting all over again. I was drinking and living on the streets again. I knew I could never go back to North Carolina. I felt awfully lonely and confused.

In November, I had what is called a grand mal seizure and was taken to Cafritz Hospital (which is now Greater Southeast Community Hospital). I was admitted for 14 days. While in the hospital, I actually saw them perform a liver biopsy on me. The doctors put a needle through my ribs and into my liver. They said that I had a bad liver. But I believe that since I was a drunk, they wanted to experiment on me.

While in the hospital, I lied and panhandled, finally raising seven dollars in less than hour. I told those I stopped that I had been stranded in DC and got sick. Some people felt sorry for me and reached in their wallets or purses to find money for me. After my release from the hospital, I went back to Deanwood. The first thing I did was buy a pint of vodka and six beers, then got drunk.

For the next six months, until the end of May 1972, I slept in the woods, in empty houses, and in abandoned cars. I ate out of trashcans. I was a skid row bum.

I was in bad shape, physically beaten up, and one foot had been broken twice. By this time, I had taken three casts off the foot. And I was in DC Detox. These people had made arrangements to get me into St. Elizabeth's— the largest mental institution on the East coast—the same place that I would return to on June 12.

At this time, I hadn't really given up. I saw it all as something that somebody else was doing. They were pushing me, trying to get me in the nut house, and I thought my wife had been responsible because she had told them that I needed to be in the nut house.

They admitted me with a broken leg (and a cane), and brought me to the east side on May 28, where all the chronics were housed. I raised hell up in there with that cane I had. They told me they could hold me for 48 hours. I raised so much hell that the doctors told them, "Turn him loose." So, they opened up the locked gates and let me out. I went out to the St. Elizabeth grounds and found two nuts talking to each other. I knew they were afraid of me, so I told them to show me to the gate. We went to the gate, and I walked through, then got on a bus.

I took the bus to Washington, DC. I was lost, and I didn't know where I was going. Somehow, I got on a bus and got out of DC, winding back up at Deanwood, where I had been "carrying the stick" and where my wife lived. I started drinking Wild Irish Rose wine and went into a blackout. It was the worst blackout I ever had.

That same night, during this blackout, I went to my wife's house with a knife and tried to stab her. My sons stopped me. That is what they tell me. You see, I have no recall of that temporary span where I seemed to others to be operating normally. I don't remember anything from the night of May 28 until June 8, the following Monday. I don't know what happened. That time was taken away from me—May 28 until June 8.

I found an empty house off East Capitol Street. It was an old government subsidy house that had been boarded up. But I got in there, and I awoke on the second floor the next morning. The sun was up. I looked up at ceiling and felt a terrible emptiness. I didn't know what to do or where to go. I wanted to die.

The record shows that when I got to St. Elizabeth's on June 12, I weighed only 149 pounds. The cast was off my leg now, so during the time between May 28 and June 8, another cast had been taken off my leg; but I don't remember when or by whom. I just remember it was gone.

That morning when I got up, I wanted to die worse than anything in the world. If I had had the money, I would have paid anybody to blow my head off. But I believe that this was the turning point—the day that everything started to change.

I managed to get back to my wife's house, which wasn't far from where I came to out of the blackout, and she called the police. The policemen carried me to DC Detox. It may have been in the evening—I don't know exactly when it was. But when I got to DC Detox, a tall white woman stood in the hallway.

"Get him out of here."

They told her that I wanted to come here.

She said, "Get him out of here."

They said, "But he wanted to come here. We did our job."

They left. When they closed the door, she stared at me, saying, "Get your black ass out of here."

So I went out of the door that the policemen used. A ramp sloped down underneath the Detox toward a brick wall. I sat with my back against that wall. I sat there, they say, for 14 hours.

While sitting there with my back against that wall, I saw an old drunken friend of mine coming toward me. He had been detoxed and released. He looked at me. "Paul, you're in bad shape; you need a drink." He was just getting out of Detox and had bought a fifth of Wild Irish

Rose wine. He drank the portion out of the neck of the bottle down to the shoulders. He said, "Drink this and maybe they'll let you in." I drank the fifth of wine and felt nothing. It was like I hadn't even drunk it. This is how I know that I had my last drink on June 8.

I continued to sit there, in and out of blackouts, until some time the next morning, when they called me in. I understand that, after I cleared up some, a conversation had been going on inside the Detox. They were saying, "He's acting differently. He's not the same. He's been there all night. He could have been gone, but he's still there, after 14 hours, so maybe we ought to look into it." They brought me back in, and I stayed there for three days. Then they released me again and gave me a token, and watched me go outside the building. They told me to go to Seventh Street to the bus stop. They told me, "Paul, if you get sober, the hardest part of your sobriety will be from here to that bus stop, because you've got to go there by yourself, without a drink, and we're not going with you."

They gave me a token. I scrambled and stumbled toward that bus stop, not drinking, shaking like a volcano, and stinking. For the entire half block, I was in a war. A voice inside me kept saying, "Don't go there." I kept fighting against that as if it were my worse enemy. It was my voice, but I was against it. I didn't want to fight it, but I knew I had to. Each step was a little battle, a skirmish against that voice. To my right, I saw all the people standing in front of the bus. Would they help me? I went up the steps of the bus and tried to put the token in the box. It fell. I tried to get it, and the bus driver said, "That's all right, don't you get it." All those people sitting in the long benches in front of the bus moved to other seats. They gave me the entire front because I was smelly and looking crazy.

When we got to St. Elizabeth's Hospital, the bus driver let me off and escorted me across the street into the gate.

Chapter 8

WE CAN ALL WALK UPRIGHT

I entered the building and went to central admissions, and they carried me back to the east side again, where all the chronics were. By this time, the fight in me was gone. I didn't resist. They brought me in without a struggle. The half-dozen staff members looked at me angrily because I had returned. I had already been there on May 28.

They ordered two guys to give me a bath. I was 35 years old, and I had drunk myself into this sad state of mind. These two big guys came down the hall and escorted me to the bathing area—a room filled with toilets, showers, and one tub. They prepared to bathe me. They took off my clothes and started spraying me with the shower hose. This was devastating—it was humiliating—it was lower than low. This is what alcohol had done to me. This is the dilemma of humiliation that we talk about in recovery.

During those days, I sat in that ward with chronically ill residents—people who couldn't even talk. They made signs and pictures. As if I were in a ghost world, I looked at their long thick tongues, hanging out almost the length of six inches. And I'm sitting there with them.

Within a month I had I dried up. I started to wonder, "What am I doing here? What did I do to get here?" One day a male attendant came by my room and said, "It could be worse." I was wondering how could it get worse. My family was gone, and here I was in the nut house where I would probably be for the rest of my life. Another day an inmate pointed to the back door, by the back screen up from the top floor and said, "That's the graveyard out there; that's your next stop."

Then treatment started. Anne Moore, an occupational therapist, approached me with a big smile. But she was a white woman, and I thought they were preparing to hang me or something. I didn't know if I had done anything wrong or not. She was too friendly. I wasn't used to people being that cordial to me. She would come up and touch me, and her fingers on my arm scared me to death.

Then one day they assigned me to an occupational therapy group designed to teach us how to accomplish practical tasks. I had forgotten everything I had ever known. The first thing I did was to make an ashtray out of a piece of tin, little marble stones and cement. They wanted to see if I could follow a line and keep coordinated. They were applying also some psychological therapy, but I didn't know it at the time. They were checking the coordination from my mind to my body. It seemed as if I was in bad shape to them.

So, we started a project that lasted about three months. We would lace a man's wallet. You had to go in and out of the holes and bind it properly. I don't know how, but I was able to accomplish that.

One of the amazing things about the treatment is that they made me get out of bed at 6 a.m. as soon as I became a patient there, and that didn't seem right to me. My foot was broken, but they gave me a mop and showed me how to maneuver myself. I held the mop and the bucket against the wall. Then I could move around to take the weight off the leg, and then swing the mop. I don't know whether I was doing any good or not, but it was intended to ease the sense of personal devastation that I was feeling.

I continued to do this over and over, every morning, mopping the hall. They kept me mopping the hall for the entire 19 months. That is all I did—just mop the hall and come in and sit down; mop the hall and come in and sit down—over and over as much as I could. Then, since I had training in barbering, they placed me in the barbershop to help cut hair. I was allowed to lather the patient and eventually use the clipper a little—but not right away. They had told the master barber not to give me a razor. Reports on me indicated that I might use sharp instruments as weapons if I got upset.

Then the real mending started. I was assigned to an occupational therapy group, consisting of a one-on-one counselor and a psychologist. They had me doing everything. I worked with blots to try to describe what they looked like. I coordinated round holes, square pegs, and square holes. This would go on for months.

Every night they took five of us out of the unit to a self-help group meeting. I wondered what this was all about, why people talked to me and tried to get others to shake my hand and see if I would talk. During these 21 months so much happened. They let me loose to see if I could stay outside the gate for an hour and come back without drinking. Eventually that leave was extended to two hours.

In my sixth month I was eligible for the system in DC that allowed you to leave an institution if you were in recovery. You could get some pretty good jobs. Several of my friends from that unit had been working for a few months.

But they wouldn't let me get a job at a decent agency or firm. They kept me mopping. They said that it was for ego and "bigshotitis" and pride's sake, and they kept me mopping. Finally, after six months, they allowed me to do some part-time work close to the hospital. I was mopping the basement floors. Even when I went off the grounds, I could only get a job mopping. I was getting pretty resentful and angry about this constraint. But their aim was to get me to be more humble so that they could communicate with me, and so that I could reach other people.

I stayed sober for a year and didn't drink on the unit. But I was always waiting for someone—a family member, an acquaintance, anybody—to come visit me. But nobody ever came, and that loneliness was difficult to deal with. I didn't understand the rejection. The counselors kept pointing out to me that this loneliness and rejection were caused by my own choices and that I had done certain things to myself. I would have to work through my feelings. And as I did, things kept getting better.

After working at the mopping job for about ten months, I was able to get a job driving an old truck for a few hours, but the paychecks bounced.

Then the hospital allowed me to take a job driving sightseeing buses for the DC Transit line for a week— long enough to observe my behavior. After watching me, in secret, drive for a few bus trips, they were fearful that I might not be far enough out of the woods. They were afraid that I might go off, scare everybody or hurt somebody, and they would have a big lawsuit to deal with. So I couldn't continue.

That was another big blow that hurt me again. Other patients were going out on pass for the weekend now, but they wouldn't let me go out. Sometimes they would let me go and sometimes they wouldn't. They knew that if they didn't give me a pass, I would get upset. When I got upset, they urged me to talk about what I was feeling.

Finally, after I had been there about 14 or 15 months, they began to talk to me about going outside to live. That scared me to death.

This was a setback emotionally because I was fearful of going through that gate and facing the outside. I just had this fear that booze was going to jump on me and control my life. I didn't want to drink now, but I had a feeling that a need to drink would overtake me. It was a phobia that I would have to do a lot of work on.

I learned a lot from the seminars about fears and phobias and how to work through those things. They were run by one of the best psychiatrists in the city. He talked often about sublimation.

I remember asking him one time, "What is this sublimation?"

He said, "It's when you get into a sticky situation and you get so frustrated that you don't know what to do." He said that you must stop, back up, and do something else that you can benefit from. Then you settle down and come back and look at the situation. The situation looks different at that point. I was trying to back up and look again at certain circumstances. But they were pushing on me pretty hard about leaving the hospital.

In August of 1973, H.B. Hutchinson Brothers Trucking Company, whose fleet featured those big yellow Mack trucks, hired me. I operated machines and was a light foreman, also. By this time, I had also started sitting in therapy groups and learning counseling skills. I was beginning to understand the pain involved in recovering without a drink. I had really come a long way, because when I first arrived at St. Elizabeth's Hospital, I was only an experimental case. By this time, I had physically recovered, and I was now working on those deep, underlying emotional problems that are the basis of alcoholism.

When I had been there 19 months, they told me it was time for me to leave. It was January 1974. I was scared to death. I started preparing to go to the next stage of my life. Then they asked me where I was going. I said that I was going home to Juanita and children.

They asked me, "Mister Austin, did they invite you to come back?"

I said, "No, they didn't invite me to come back."

They said, "Then how do you know she wants you to come there? We've been trying to get your wife involved in your recovery here for a long time, and she has always refused. She doesn't want any parts of you or your recovery."

So I went home anyway, against the hospital's advice and against my better judgment. I was able to stay at home with my children and Juanita for four months. They didn't seem to accept me. It felt awfully cold. They just avoided me—hardly speaking, not expressing any interest in what I was doing, sometimes just ignoring me. Looking back, I understand now what their concerns were. They had fears and negative memories about what I had put them through.

I had gone through hell not drinking, and I didn't want anything to drink now. But learning how to deal with these changes at age 37 was a challenge that was almost devastating to me. I had a job and an old second-hand car, and it dawned on me one day that I was going to get drunk. I could feel that right down in the pit of my guts. I knew that I was going to drink. Juanita told me every day that I was going to drink again. That didn't help me either.

What did I do? I decided that before I drank again I would go back to the hospital and tell them that something was wrong. One of the counselors told me, "We were sure that you would come back, but we thought you would be drunk." They kept me for two months. And in these two months, I learned more about myself and what treatment meant than I did during the entire 19 months I was there. Why? I was finally ready to let them get inside my guts and my head.

I became upset about some things a patient who had been there only two months said to me. His saying that I was almost worthless hurt me badly. I broke out of the hospital, bought a knife and came back with the intent of harming him to get even. Several of the staff interrupted me, forced me into an office to talk. They pointed out the insanity of my behavior. "If you don't do something about your anger, we will send you to the prison at Lorton," they warned. This was the key, in June 1974. Two weeks after this episode, I gave up the knife and I haven't carried one since.

That knife was a complex part of the fears I had. It shielded me from doing what I had to do for myself. Learning about the connection between my fears and my anger was a significant victory for me.

I spent a total of 21 months in St. Elizabeth's Hospital, much of it in therapy groups. Some of the tests indicated that I had the ability to lead people. One of the counselors told me, "There's a lot of nuts running up and down here looking for you. They want to talk to you." My potential for actually helping others frightened me a bit.

In the same conversation he asked, "What do you want to do when you really get free—if you get free— from the hospital?" I didn't know it then, but he was setting me up to learn how to work with people who have my kind of illness.

I said, "Well, I'd like to go back to singing." I thought that would impress him. But it didn't.

He said, "Where were those people you sang with when we first found you?" He suggested that if I associated myself with alcoholics, I would have a good chance of staying sober. Plus, he felt that those drunks would listen to me. So I started on the road to becoming a counselor. And that's where I've been ever since. That is how I got involved in Montgomery County volunteer services.

In early 1974, after being in St. Elizabeth's Hospital for 21 months, I earned convalescent leave. I returned home to live with my family, and that's where challenging problems began to surface. They did not understand alcoholism and the need to accept it as an illness. They had been hurt deeply by me, mentally and emotionally. But Juanita did not accept the fact that she and the kids also had their own emotional issues to confront. After two-and-one-half years, she finally began to attend self-help groups for herself. But the kids never attended any groups. I think they just avoided dealing with what I saw as neurotic behavior. They would survive, over a period of time, through the growing-up process.

Since I was convinced that staying associated with this illness was a key component of recovery, I participated in an aftercare group for two years. Every other week I attended counseling meetings each night. I also worked with self-help groups and was made chairman of one.

Every other Saturday night I took on a commitment at DC Detox. I now accepted myself as a skid-row bum and alcoholic without reservation, deep down in my gut.

It was also in 1974 that my sponsor began talking about my past. He reminded me that I had caused many problems for myself and others, and that I would have to clean it all up. My God, wasn't I dealing with enough uncertainty already? He talked about all the broken promises I had made, the physical damage I had done, and the bills I had not made restitution for. The mental and emotional problems I had caused my family and loved ones would all have to be cleaned up for me to be a free man. That way, I would not go through life looking over my shoulder. He reminded me that it is difficult to remain sober and paranoid at the same time. Listening to him reminded me of how anyone trying to get sober without a sponsor is plodding uphill. Through all the problems and fears I had to face, my sponsor was there with me. We had a great relationship. He loved me very much simply because I was a skid-row bum. I was also teachable.

In the next two years, my life seemed to be changing faster than I could have ever expected.

In August 1975, I was asked to go into Montgomery County, Maryland, and begin training as a volunteer counselor. The 12 white and one black client caused me some apprehension, and I came down with neurodermatitis—very unstable emotional reactions.

In February 1976, I became a part-time counselor for the county. I was on my way to recovery despite the pain eating at me. But my sponsor was there with me. He would say to me, "Paul, the cowards won't start, the weak would fall by the way, and it would be only a few of us who would make it to the end." The fellowship we enjoyed took second place to nothing or nobody.

I was employed for 20 months as a part-time counselor before becoming a full-time employed staff member. A senior counselor, Clyde, taught me a great deal. In 1978, he died, and I became the only black counselor of a staff of 26 at this Montgomery County facility in Maryland. I had to deal with a number of stressful discrimination issues.

In April, I was injured in a trucking company accident and received a monetary settlement of $28,000 in 1979. I bought my first house. By this time, my family had assessed our situation differently. Being sober, I was able to look at matters with a changed perspective, especially since I was now a part of things rather than apart from things. I saw all my children graduate from high school.

Then I had another reminder that alcohol kills. In August 1983, another brother, a skid-row bum, died in Carthage, North Carolina. He had known and seen me sober many times before he passed on. He had respected me highly for battling alcoholism, and would ask from time to time if I minded his drinking. I would say no, because I understood then that all of us just don't make it. He led a lonely life and was buried next to my father. There had been six boys and six girls in my family; now there were only two boys left—my younger brother and I. And he suffers from an inflamed pancreas caused by alcohol.

In April 1983, I was transferred to Rockville where I worked with services treating driving-while-intoxicated cases.

In 1984, I resigned my job at the Montgomery County facility to work at St. Elizabeth's Hospital in the substance abuse treatment program as a counselor. Here I was being hired at St. Elizabeth's Hospital where I had once been a patient. I worked in this program for 18 months. In the meantime, I was putting together a dream I had. I founded and developed an outpatient program for alcohol counseling services in March 1985. I now have 11 employees consisting of four counselors, one medical doctor, one attorney, one administrative assistant, and three Ph.D. psychologists. Several volunteers work in the program, also.

In these 22 years of sobriety, I have experienced a great deal. I had a home and two lots willed to me in Florida. I bought a new mobile home in North Carolina and two lots, and even own a home in Prince George's

County, Maryland. I have been asked to set up an outpatient treatment program in North Carolina—the same state that chained me up in 1971 and ordered me never to return. It's a possibility.

To anyone who is fighting alcohol and wants to be sober, I say without any hesitation that it is not easy. Do not listen to all that stuff you hear and read. My formula for winning the battle has several components. You must go to meetings, pray to God, and help someone else with no strings attached. You must find someone to whom you can bare your soul. That baring will help you get in touch with yourself and all the pent-up emotions you carry around. My worst problems could be traced back easily to my own instinctive feelings.

I will be just fine by taking one day at a time of not drinking. I must always know where God's place is in my life, and remember that I'm not He. Today, I have friends, real ones, and I'm walking upright—just as God intended me to do in the first place. If there is one message I would leave you with, it is that He intends for each of us to walk upright.

I wish my three brothers, who were lost to alcoholism, could have benefited the way I have. I am sober now. God's will has been done.